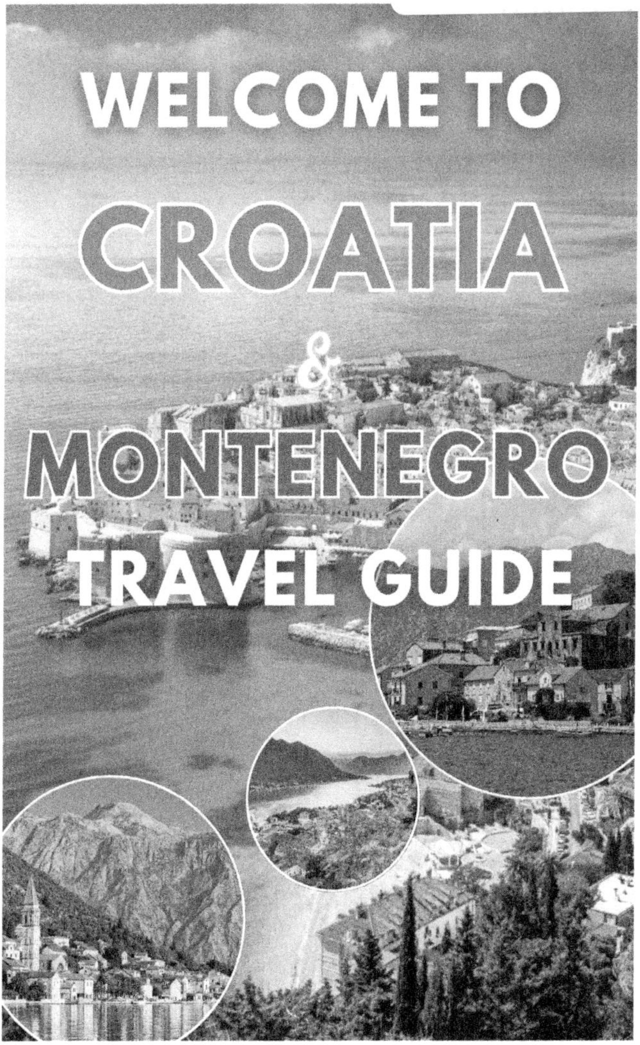

WELCOME TO CROATIA & MONTENEGRO TRAVEL GUIDE

Table Of Content

Chapter 1 – Introduction to the Adriatic Gems........5
    1.1 Understanding the Croatia & Montenegro Experience........6
    1.2 Geography, Climate, and Seasons...........12
    What This Means for You........20
    1.3 Travel Logistics: Visas, Currency, Health..22
    1.4 Best Times to Visit and How to Avoid Crowds........29

Chapter 2 – Planning & Budgeting Smartly..........35
    2.1 Setting a Realistic Daily Budget...............35
    2.2 Choosing Your Travel Style......................40
    2.3 Transportation Options: Flights, Ferries, Buses, Rental Cars..........46
    2.4 Apps and Resources for Smart Planning..52

Chapter 3: Castles & Capitals — Urban Highlights...59
    3.1 Zagreb to Ljubljana Day Trip.....................60
    3.2 Split: Diocletian's Palace & Seaside Vibes...64
    3.3 Dubrovnik's City Walls & Storytelling Heritage..........67
    3.4 Kotor & the Bay of Kotor Towns...............75

Chapter 4 – Islands & Coastal Routes.................83
    4.1 Island-Hopping Basics: Ferry Logistics.....84
    4.2 Hvar, Korčula & Brač Highlights................90

4.3 Montenegro's Hidden Coastal Gems: Perast & Sveti Stefan... 96
4.4 Scenic Drives & Coastal Walks.............. 101
Chapter 5 – National Parks & Nature Trails........ 109
5.1 Plitvice & Krka Waterfalls (Croatia)......... 110
5.2 Paklenica & Lakeside Hikes.................... 115
5.3 Durmitor & Tara Canyon (Montenegro)... 122
5.4 Lake Skadar & Biodiversity Trails........... 127
Chapter 6 – Adventure & Outdoor Thrills............ 134
6.1 Kayaking & Paddleboarding.................... 135
6.2 Mountain Biking and Rock Climbing....... 140
6.3 Zip-lining, Rafting, and Cave Tours......... 144
6.4 Coastal Sailing and Diving...................... 149
Chapter 7 – Culture & Authentic Experiences.... 155
7.1 Festivals, Music, and Local Traditions.... 156
7.2 Historical Depth: Roman, Venetian, Ottoman Legacies....................................... 160
7.3 Art, Galleries & Film Events.................... 164
7.4 Learning from Locals, Community Tourism... 169
Chapter 8 – Food, Wine & Local Flavors............ 174
8.1 Croatian Seafood, Truffles & Olive Oil Trails. 175
8.2 Montenegrin Rakija, Wines & Cheeses.. 179
8.3 Markets, Street Food & Vegan Options.. 182
8.4 Winery and Brewery Tours..................... 186
Chapter 9 – Where to Stay................................. 191
9.1 Choosing Hotels, Villas, Guesthouses.... 192
9.2 Camping, Glamping & Eco-Lodges........ 195
9.3 Insider Booking Tips & Peak-Season

3

Strategies..199
9.4 Family & Solo-Traveler Accommodations.....204

Chapter 10 – On the Road: Itineraries...............209
10.1 Seven-Day Coastal Highlights.............. 210
10.2 Ten-Day Croatia + Montenegro Journey.....214
10.3 Build-Your-Own Adventure: Pick & Mix. 217
10.4 Short Breaks and Thematic Routes...... 221

Chapter 11 – Safety, Health & Practical Advice.. 225
11.1 Staying Safe in Cities and Nature......... 226
11.2 Getting Around: Driving Rules, Ferries..231
11.3 Health, Insurance & Emergencies..........237
11.4 Locals' Etiquette and Cultural Norms....242

Chapter 12 – Seasonal Insights & Packing.........247
12.1 Packing for Seaside & Mountain...........248
12.2 Dressing for Festivals and Culture........252
12.3 Seasonal Pros/Cons: Off-Season Tips. 256
12.4 Eco-Friendly Gear Checklist................ 261

Chapter 13: Beyond the Map – Insider Tips........266
13.1 Budget Hacks & Tourist-Tax Strategies.267
13.2 Photo-Worthy Spots & Hidden Viewpoints..273
13.3 Volunteer Travel & Giving Back............ 276
13.4 Future-Proof Travel Amid Rising Tourism...281

Conclusion..286
Recap Your Priorities: What Kind of Trip Are You Planning?..287
Personalize Your Experience: Make It Yours 288
Go Deeper—and Come Back...................... 289

Final Thoughts: Traveling Light, Leaving a Gentle Footprint.. 290
Appendix... 292
    A. Transit & Ferry Schedules....................... 292
    B. Packing Checklist & Gear Guide.............. 296
    C. Emergency Contacts & Useful Apps......... 299

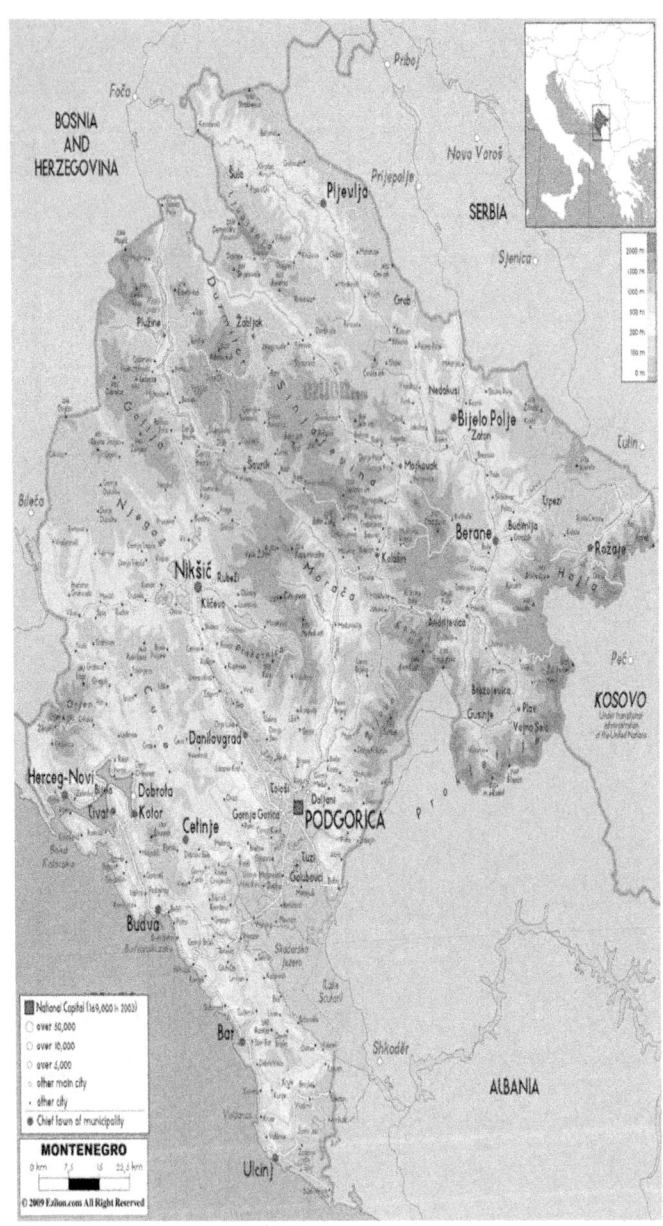

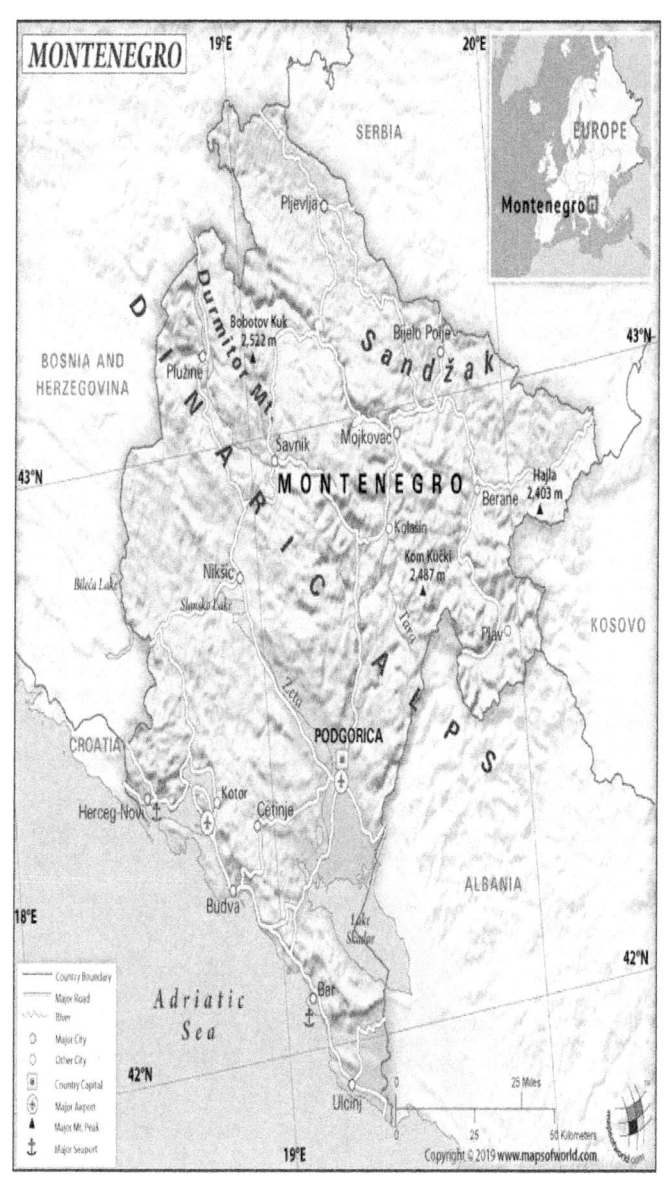

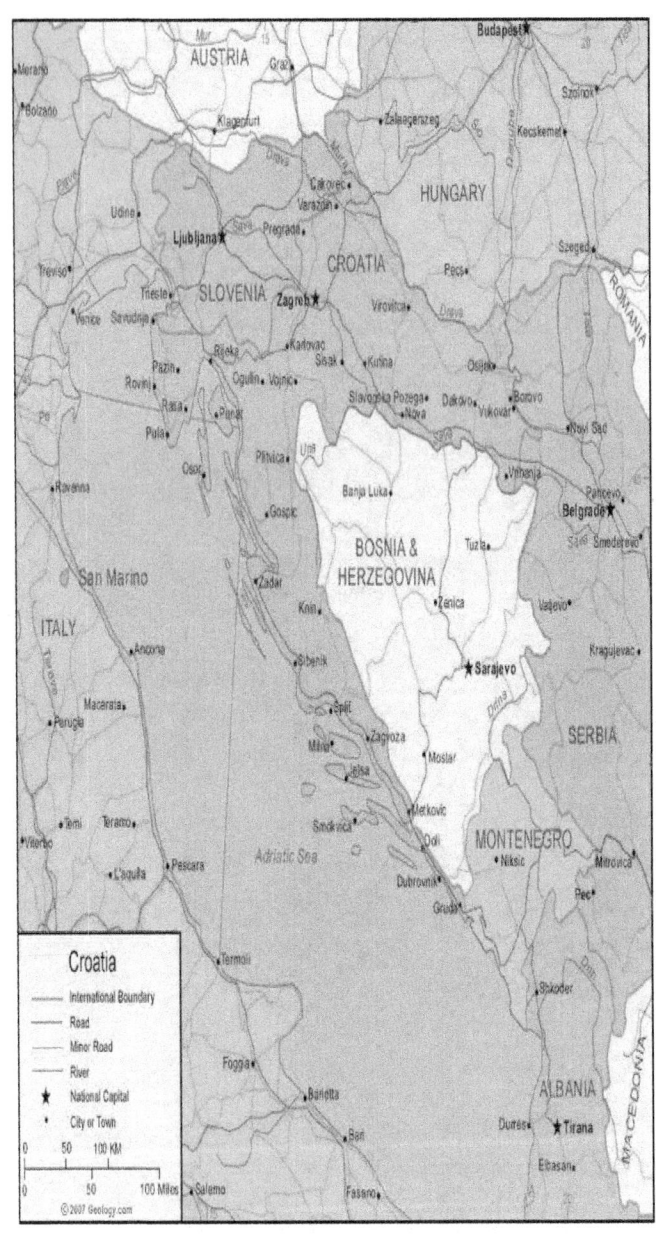

Chapter 1 – Introduction to the Adriatic Gems

Tucked between Central Europe and the Balkans, Croatia and Montenegro share more than a coastline. These two countries offer a rich blend of cultures, landscapes, and histories that stretch well beyond their postcard-perfect views. This chapter lays the groundwork for understanding what makes this region so special—from the natural rhythms of life along the Adriatic to the practicalities of getting around.

Whether you're curious about medieval towns clinging to cliffs, winding coastal roads perfect for a slow drive, or the quiet charm of inland villages, this introduction will help you travel more intentionally. We'll look at what defines the Croatia and Montenegro experience, how geography and climate shape the way locals live and visitors move, and how to plan your trip with timing, visas, and logistics in mind.

1.1 Understanding the Croatia & Montenegro Experience

Coastal Rhythm and Mediterranean Character

At the heart of the Adriatic experience is the sea. Along both Croatian and Montenegrin shores, life unfolds with the ebb and flow of the tide. Morning light bathes ancient limestone walls, café tables fill with locals drinking coffee and making small talk, and ferries depart for neighboring islands and coastal towns. Come afternoon, the pace slows: shutters close, streets empty, and lunch stretches luxuriously. Evenings bring a vibrant revival—plazas light up, tavernas hum with conversation, and waves lap against stone promenades.

Pretend you're staying in a centuries-old Adriatic town—say, Hvar, Korčula, or Perast. Each has its own micro-culture:

- Hvar (Croatia): Tourists flock for its nightlife, yet the morning remains unspoiled. By 10 a.m., fishermen unload fresh catch on the waterfront, and lavender fields above the hill-mapped old town cast fragrant breezes. Long lunches are common, followed by siesta, then cocktails as the sun fades.

- Perast (Montenegro): A place of quiet grandeur—navy-blue bay waters, white bell towers, and Baroque mansions. Cruise ships loom on the horizon, but inside the town, it's peaceful. People dine early—around 7 p.m.—and earthen tones of the bay glow under lanterns.

These coastal towns reflect centuries of Venetian, Ottoman, and Austro-Hungarian influences—a complex architectural palimpsest. Renaissance palaces butt up against Ottoman domes. Cuisine blends Mediterranean simplicity—olive oil, fresh fish—with Balkan heartiness—smoked cheese, roast lamb.

Inland Depth and Highland Traditions

The coastline tells one story; the hinterland writes another. Leave the sea's edge and you enter a quieter, earthier world. In Croatia, driving inland brings you into karst landscapes—magical limestone fields laced with rivers, sinkholes, caves. You'll find remote hamlets where time feels slower; where church bells mark midday, and farmers tend sheep on cleared stone terraces. Peka (meat and vegetables slow-cooked under a bell cover) is common here, a dish meant for sharing.

In Montenegro, the interior is even more dramatic. The Dinaric Alps tower over villages like Žabljak near Durmitor, where locals lead you to mountain pastures for cheese and honey sampling. Orthodox monasteries cling to steep cliffs; old women in traditional dress weave carpets or sell honey and herbs at roadside stands. This region's heart beats slower, shaped by centuries of self-reliance, wood-working, shepherding, and folk music.

Understanding both coastal and inland rhythms helps you shape your trip. Want nightlife and glamour? Head coast. Craving solitude and nature? Go inland. Yet the real magic often lies between: driving mountain passes to feel the transition shift as you descend toward the Adriatic—seeing how landscapes, dialects, and dining tables change in just a couple of hours.

Culture: A Crossroads of Influences

Croatia is predominantly Roman Catholic, Montenegro mostly Orthodox Christian; yet both countries have Muslim communities along the coast, a legacy of Ottoman rule. Easter might be marked by midnight church services in Split, Orthodox celebrations in Cetinje, and iftar in coastal towns during Ramadan. This diversity colors celebrations, festivals, greetings, and even the food.

In Dubrovnik, you'll pass by bell towers chiming for Mass, and a few blocks away, mosques or modern Islamic centers. In Sarajevo—close enough for a day trip—you'll glimpse all three religions and their coexistence.

Language can reflect history's layering. In Istria (Croatia), signs might be in Croatian, Italian, and sometimes Slovenian. Locals might speak dialects blending Slavic grammar with Venetian words. In Montenegro, you'll hear Montenegrin (almost identical to Serbian/Bosnian/Croatian), but some older folk cling to Ottoman-era Turkish words, while Albanian is common near the southern border.

Cuisine: A Regional Story on Your Plate

Picture your plate as a map. On the coast, expect grilled Adriatic fish, sardines, shellfish, olive oil, and capers, usually served simply—lemon, herbs, and maybe aioli. Inland gets richer: kouzina becomes hearty—mountain cheese, meats, root vegetables, chestnuts.

Breakfast in coastal towns might be burek (pastry filled with cheese or meat), accompanied by yogurt or ayran. By lunch, you're more likely indulging in fresh-caught amberjack with a side of blitva (Swiss chard and potatoes) in a local konoba (tavern). Dinner flows late—just as the sun is setting—and goes for hours, with wine, rakija, and conversation.

In the interior, dishes like janjetina (roast lamb) appear in stone village restaurants alongside homemade rakija served in shot glasses. Sweets may come as priganice (fried dough), sometimes drizzled with honey or topped with cheese.

Beyond the Border: Shared Rhythms, Different Voices

Though Croatia and Montenegro have different national identities, travelers often find their experiences echoing each other. Durmitor in Montenegro and Plitvice or Krka in Croatia all showcase nature that feels wild yet accessible. Coastal villages—from Split to Tivat—share the same string of limestone roofs and waterfront cafes. Festivals in both places reflect shared histories: Orthodox celebrations, Catholic saints' days, even traditional music and food.

Your Croatian driver may reminisce about fishing trips in Boka Bay (Montenegro), while Montenegrins mention holidaying on Hvar. The cross-border cultural dialogue predates modern boundaries: identity here is fluid—coastal folk are less keen to draw lines between nations than inland towns.

Reflecting on Pace and Presence

My point is this: traveling here isn't about ticking off "must-sees." It's about noticing rhythm—the speed of life, the clink of wine glasses at 11 a.m., the shift from polished towns to forgotten mountain hamlets. It's about being present, curious, flexible enough to ask locals what they love—where they fish, what they grow, where to eat beyond TripAdvisor.

Chapter 1 is meant to give you context on what shapes that rhythm so you can travel not just smart—but whole-heartedly. Embrace slowdown, expect surprises, taste deeply, and let the Adriatic guide your tempo.

1.2 Geography, Climate, and Seasons

Mapping the Land: What You See, Where You Go

Take a moment and picture the coast on a map. Croatia stretches north-south along the eastern Adriatic but swerves around Bosnia and Herzegovina, creating a fragmented, finger-like edge peppered with hundreds of islands. Montenegro, just south, is shorter—about half the length—but packed into a tight, mountainous wedge with a deeply indented coastline.

Coastlines and Islands

- Croatia's coast: rugged cliffs, pebble-and-sand beaches, historic ports. Over a thousand islands rise from the sea; about fifty are inhabited with regular ferry service. Kissed by lavender, olive groves, and pine forests, each island—from quiet Mljet to boisterous Hvar—feels distinct.

- Montenegro's coast: shorter but dramatic. The Bay of Kotor curves inward, surrounded by steep mountains that rise from the water like islands themselves. Budva, Petrovac, and Herceg Novi break the coast into sheltered beaches and rugged cliffs. There are few true islands here; instead, you get fjord-like vistas and deep bays.

Driving the coast is not a straight line. Some routes take you inland over switchback-laden roads before cliffside curves—roads hugging oceans on one side, mountains on the other. Public buses, ferries, and car rentals are all options, but expect travel times to stretch because of curves.

Inland Terrain and National Parks

- Croatia beyond the shore: Move inland about 30–100 kilometers to find karst plateaus, forested sections, and national parks like Plitvice Lakes, Paklenica, or Risnjak. The terrain is less settled, cooler, with fewer tourists but richer in waterfalls and hiking trails. The land turns wilder as you reach Lika or Gorski Kotar—perfect for a road trip into nature.

- Montenegro's interior: dominated by the Dinaric Alps. Northern areas like Durmitor National Park include jagged peaks, canyons, and glacial lakes. Monasteries perch on cliffs, sheep grazed crags, and villages cling to roads that snake up into the sky.

Borders, Distances, and Accessibility

Travelers often underestimate how far things are "as the crow flies." Dubrovnik to Žabljak, for instance, might look close—it's under a hundred kilometers—but the journey involves two border crossings, coastal roads, a tunnel, and a few mountain passes. Travel time could be four to six hours.

Plan accordingly. Allow buffer days when moving from coast to mountains. Whether you rent a car or use buses, realistic travel windows are key—especially if you want calm in Kotor and solitude in Durmitor without rushing.

Climate Patterns: What to Expect

The region's geography creates climate variety—Mediterranean along the shore, continental and Alpine inland, and microclimates scattered throughout.

Coastal Mediterranean Climate

- Summer (June–August): Hot and dry. Temperatures can reach 30–35°C (86–95°F). Humidity is low, and sea breezes often keep things comfortable. Beaches and towns become crowded, ferries book quickly, and restaurants fill early.

- Shoulder seasons—Spring (April–May), Fall (September–October): Golden seasons. Daytime temps hover between 20–25°C (68–77°F), sea water warms enough for swimming (especially after June), vineyards are lush, and evenings are comfortable for strolling. Rain is possible but usually in short bursts. Tourist services are fully operational but less packed.

- Winter (November–March): Mild but damp. Daytime temps hover around

7–13°C (45–55°F). Rain is common; snow is rare along the coast. Island hotels may close for the season, but towns like Dubrovnik and Split remain open, offering a peaceful off-season charm.

Inland and Mountain Climate

- Lowland Interior: Largely continental. Hot summers (though less intense than the coast) and cold winters. Snow may fall, but usually melts quickly. Spring grows greenery; fall offers colorful foliage.

- Mountainous Interior: Alpine conditions. In summer, days remain pleasantly warm (18–25°C / 65–77°F), but nights can dip below 10°C (50°F). Winter brings real snow—ideal for skiing at Durmitor or Platak. Shoulder seasons bring unpredictable weather—rain, fog, even late snow.

Microclimates and Local Quirks

- Bay of Kotor: Broadly Mediterranean, but with more humidity. Mornings can begin misty, and thunderstorms are more frequent. This microclimate nourishes dense vegetation—citrus trees, palms, magnolias—in contrast with rocky Dalmatia.

- Island Interiors: Elevated inland sections of bigger islands like Brač or Korčula are cooler than coastlines; may surprise with evening chill and fog even in summer.

- Canyon Gorges: Places like Tara Canyon (Montenegro) or Velebit Mountains (Croatia) can trap cold air. Expect cooler temps, rapid weather changes, and thick forest cover.

Seasonal Planning: What to Pack, What to Do

Packing by Season

- Summer: Light clothing—shorts, dresses, tees—plus sun protection. But bring a light sweater or shawl for seaside breezes or mountain nights. Beach gear: swimsuit, flip-flops, quick-dry towel, water shoes for rocky beaches. Closed-toe shoes are a must for walking on uneven paths or stable castles.

- Spring/Fall: Layering is key—shorts or pants, tees, long-sleeve shirts, rain jacket, travel scarf. On islands, wind can bite in spring. Bring a sweater or fleece for mountain dips.

- Winter: Coastal winter can be wet and chilly. Think waterproof mid-layer, umbrella, warm long-sleeve shirt. For mountains: thermal base layers, insulated jacket, fleece, gloves, hat. Snow boots if you're headed to ski regions.

Best Times for Specific Travel Styles

- Island-hopping & swimming: Late May to early October. Sea temperature warms by June; offshore water stays until late September.

- Hiking & rural exploration: Spring (May–June) and autumn (September–October) are prime. Trails open early, wildflowers abound in spring, and fall brings color. Tourist crowds have thinned.

- Photography & sightseeing: Spring and fall offer better light, fewer tourists, and mild weather.

Golden-hour photos in Dubrovnik or Kotor are more rewarding without throngs.

- Winter sports: December through March in the mountains. Some ski resorts open, though snow cover varies. Paths for snowshoeing, cross-country skiing, and winter hikes remain accessible.

Timing Festivals & Cultural Events

Each season brings cultural resonance:

- Summer festivals (June–August): Dubrovnik Summer Festival (classical music and theater), Hvar's fishing festivals, Budva Carnival.

- Religious celebrations: Orthodox Easter often falls in April; Catholic Easter earlier in spring. Coastal towns celebrate patron saints (e.g., Dubrovnik on May 22—St. Blaise, Hvar on August 15—Assumption of Mary).

- Winter traditions: Orthodox Christmas (January 7), New Year's concerts in Zagreb, Dubrovnik, and Herceg Novi, and Orthodox New Year on January 14.

Navigating the Unexpected

A hiker in Plitvice might escape early summer crowds, only to be caught in an unexpected thunderstorm off-season. Or your drive to Kotor might be slowed by thick fog rolling in unexpected valleys. When traveling here:

1. Build slack into your schedule. Days often double as transition times.

2. Check local weather forecasts. Mountain weather can change fast. Even coastal mornings might bring fog.

3. Plan for variable dining hours. Winter hours vary; off-season, villages may have only one café open—and close early.

4. Have backup lodging. A small inn might shut during low season. Confirm ahead and carry phone numbers.

What This Means for You

- Choose your theme. Are you after beach life, mountain solitude, or a mix? Let the seasons guide you.

- Pack in layers. Even in summer, mornings and nights can surprise you, especially inland.

- Plan travel times carefully. Google Maps will lie here—mountain roads and ferry waits extend travel.

- Match season to activities. Want remote beaches? Go off-season. Want full services? Go shoulder season. Want festivals? Go summer.

This deeper layer of geography and climate gives you more than a glance—it's your blueprint for timing, packing, and planning effectively. You'll know where to go, when, and how to best experience each facet of Croatia and Montenegro—from orchard terraces in Istria to hidden coves on Montenegrin peninsulas.

1.3 Travel Logistics: Visas, Currency, Health

Before you can dive into the coastal towns, national parks, and cobbled old cities, you'll need to understand the nuts and bolts of traveling to and through Croatia and Montenegro. These details—visas, border crossings, money, health care—aren't glamorous, but getting them right can make the difference between smooth sailing and a stressful detour. Here's what you should know.

Visa Requirements and Entry Rules

Croatia and Montenegro are both located in Southeast Europe, but their border policies differ slightly—and they're in different stages of integration with the European Union.

Croatia

Croatia joined the Schengen Area in January 2023, meaning that travelers from Schengen countries can move freely in and out without border checks. For most tourists, especially from Europe, North America, Australia, New Zealand, and Japan, no visa is required for stays up to 90 days in any 180-day period.

If you're entering from outside the Schengen Area (e.g., the UK or the US), your 90-day allowance counts across all Schengen countries, not just Croatia. So if you've already spent time in, say, Italy or Austria before arriving in Croatia, those days count against your total.

Montenegro

Montenegro is not part of the Schengen Area, but its visa policy is fairly liberal. Citizens of the EU, UK, US, Canada, Australia, and many others can enter visa-free for up to 90 days. However, Schengen time does not count here, which is a useful trick for travelers watching the Schengen clock. If your Schengen time is up, you can hop over the border and reset in Montenegro.

Important Tip: Always check the latest visa rules before you go. Political shifts can impact border regulations quickly. Both Croatia and Montenegro allow extensions in special cases, but these must be requested well before your 90 days expire.

Crossing the Border Between Croatia and Montenegro

The border between the two is straightforward but can get congested, especially in summer. If you're traveling by car or bus, expect longer wait times near Herceg Novi (Montenegro) and Dubrovnik (Croatia). Delays of 30–60 minutes are common in peak season, sometimes longer.

If you're on foot or biking, crossings are usually quicker—but make sure the specific border crossing point allows pedestrian or bicycle transit (not all do).

Documents You'll Need:

- A valid passport with at least 3–6 months left

- Proof of onward travel (rarely checked, but good to have)

- Proof of accommodation or travel plans (again, not usually asked for)

- Travel insurance (not mandatory but strongly recommended)

Currency: What You'll Spend, Where, and How

Croatia and Montenegro each use different currencies, and while you'll find increasing use of cards and mobile payments, cash still plays a central role, especially outside major cities.

Croatia: Euro (€)

Since January 2023, Croatia officially uses the euro. ATMs are widespread and generally safe to use, especially at reputable bank branches. Avoid standalone "convenience" ATMs with high fees and poor exchange rates—these are common in tourist zones.

Expect to use euros in:

- All hotels, restaurants, ferries, and transport systems
- Farmers markets, bakeries, and small shops
- Parking meters and public transport kiosks

Contactless payment (via credit card or phone) is standard in cities like Zagreb,

Split, and Dubrovnik, but carry cash in smaller towns, on islands, and for local buses or beach vendors.

Montenegro: Euro (€)

Though not a member of the EU, Montenegro also uses the euro as its de facto currency. There's no need to exchange again at the border if you're coming from Croatia.

Most places accept cards, especially in tourist-heavy zones like Kotor or Budva. However, rural inns, small cafes, roadside produce stands, and family-run accommodations often prefer or only accept cash.

ATMs in Montenegro: Reliable and common in urban areas, but fewer in remote villages or mountain zones. If heading inland, withdraw in advance and bring small denominations—€5, €10, €20. Large bills can be hard to break in small establishments.

Tips on Money Use

- Tipping is customary but casual: 5–10% is standard in restaurants; round up for taxis or bar tabs.

- Currency exchanges exist, but ATMs usually offer better rates. If exchanging cash, use official exchange offices (marked "mjenjačnica" in Croatian).

- Avoid dynamic currency conversion on card machines; always choose to pay in euros instead of your home currency.

Health Care, Insurance, and Medical Support

No one wants to think about getting sick on vacation, but being prepared will save stress if something goes wrong. Fortunately, both countries offer solid basic medical care, though standards and accessibility vary between urban and rural areas.

Croatia

Croatia's health care system is public and affordable, especially compared to North American costs. EU citizens with a European Health Insurance Card (EHIC) can access many services for free or reduced rates.

- Pharmacies ("ljekarna") are common and well-stocked. Staff usually speak English and can advise on minor issues.

- Emergency care is available in public hospitals. In larger cities (Split, Zagreb, Dubrovnik), some doctors speak English. In smaller towns, you may need help from your hotel or a local contact to translate.

- Private clinics are available and cost more but often offer faster service for travelers.

Montenegro

Montenegro also has public hospitals and private clinics, though infrastructure is generally less developed than Croatia. In cities like Podgorica and Kotor, you'll find English-speaking doctors and decent facilities.

- Pharmacies are marked with a green cross and easy to find.

- In rural areas, emergency care is more limited, and ambulance services may take time to arrive.

- Some private clinics cater specifically to tourists and expats—particularly near Kotor, Budva, and Herceg Novi.

Health Tips for Travelers

- Drinkable tap water: Safe to drink in both countries, though bottled water is preferred by locals in some areas due to taste.

- Travel insurance: Strongly recommended. Make sure it includes medical evacuation and emergency transport—especially if you're planning outdoor activities in remote areas.

- Vaccinations: None are required for entry. Make sure your routine vaccines (tetanus, hepatitis A/B) are up to date.

Emergencies

- Croatia emergency number: 112 (for all emergencies)

- Montenegro emergency number: 124 (ambulance), 122 (police), 123 (fire)

1.4 Best Times to Visit and How to Avoid Crowds

One of the most common mistakes travelers make when planning a trip to Croatia and Montenegro is assuming the experience is the same year-round. It's not. Summer might offer postcard-perfect days, but it also brings dense crowds, high prices, and full bookings. Knowing when—and where—to go can turn your trip from good to unforgettable.

Peak Season: July–August

This is the busiest and most expensive time to visit both countries. It's also when most festivals happen, beaches are buzzing, and every café seems to spill onto the street with life.

- Weather: Hot, dry, and sunny. Highs in the 30–35°C (86–95°F) range.

- Crowds: Expect shoulder-to-shoulder foot traffic in old towns like

Dubrovnik, Kotor, and Hvar.

- Prices: Accommodation and flights peak. Booking early is essential—often 3–6 months in advance.

- Activities: Everything is open—ferries run frequently, restaurants stay open late, and nightlife is in full swing.

When to go in peak season (if you must):

- Visit popular places early in the morning or late at night.

- Avoid weekends when cruise ships and tour buses flood old towns.

- Head to lesser-known islands (e.g., Lastovo, Vis, or Šipan in Croatia) or Montenegro's inland areas for a break from the crowds.

Shoulder Seasons: May–June and September–October

This is the sweet spot for most travelers. The weather is lovely, most businesses are open, and crowds are lighter.

- Weather: Mild and comfortable. The sea is swimmable by late May and well into October.

- Crowds: Manageable. You can explore cities like Split or Kotor without constant bottlenecks.

- Prices: Lower than summer. You'll often find good deals on accommodations, especially in September.

- Activities: Hiking, kayaking, wine tasting, and scenic drives are perfect during this time.

Tips for these seasons:

- Avoid Easter and school holidays, which can temporarily drive up demand.

- Pack layers: days are warm, but evenings can get cool, especially inland or in the mountains.

Off-Season: November–April

Tourism drops off sharply after October, especially on the islands. This season isn't for beachgoers, but it's ideal for those looking for quiet cities, lower prices, and authentic local life.

- Weather: Coastal areas are mild but rainy; inland and mountain regions can be cold and snowy.

- Crowds: Almost nonexistent—perfect if you want Dubrovnik's walls or Kotor's streets to yourself.

- Prices: Lowest of the year. You can often find boutique hotels at half the summer rate.

- Activities: Explore cultural sites, enjoy winter hikes, or try skiing in Montenegro's Durmitor or Bjelasica regions.

Caveats:

- Many island services shut down. Ferries run less often; restaurants may close for the season.

- Daylight hours are shorter; plan sightseeing accordingly.

Smart Strategies to Avoid Crowds Year-Round

Even in high season, there are ways to carve out peace and space.

- Start your days early: Get to popular attractions before 9 a.m. and you'll beat the rush—and the heat.

- Choose your base wisely: Stay in smaller towns or nearby villages and day trip to hotspots. For example, base yourself in Cavtat instead of Dubrovnik or in Prčanj instead of Kotor.

- Avoid cruise ship schedules: Both Dubrovnik and Kotor publish cruise timetables online. Plan visits when fewer ships are docked.

- Explore inland: Most tourists hug the coast. Consider visiting places like

Konavle, Cetinje, or the Pelješac peninsula.

- Travel midweek: Flights and accommodations tend to be quieter and cheaper Tuesday–Thursday.

Chapter 2 – Planning & Budgeting Smartly

Introduction

Croatia and Montenegro may be two of the most rewarding destinations in Europe, but making the most of your trip depends a lot on how well you plan—especially when it comes to money, timing, and comfort. This chapter gives you the tools to travel smart, whether you're aiming to keep things affordable or treat yourself to something more upscale.

You'll find honest breakdowns of daily travel costs, tips on balancing quality with budget, and advice on choosing a travel style that fits your personality and your wallet. We'll also walk through transportation options and point out tools that can help simplify your planning process, without pushing you toward one-size-fits-all solutions.

2.1 Setting a Realistic Daily Budget

There's no universal "right amount" to spend in Croatia or Montenegro. Your budget depends on your travel style, the season, and which regions you visit. A day in Dubrovnik's Old Town in July will cost more than a day in inland Montenegro in October. That said, it's entirely possible to have a meaningful experience on a modest budget—or to elevate it with strategic splurges.

Understanding the Range

Let's sketch out three rough travel tiers: budget, mid-range, and luxury. These are meant as starting points, not rigid boxes.

- Budget travelers can get by on €40–70 per day by staying in hostels or private rooms, eating local meals, using public transport, and prioritizing free or low-cost experiences like hikes, beaches, and city walks.

- Mid-range travelers should plan for around €90–150 per day. This allows for boutique stays, a mix of local and sit-down dining, rental car or ferry travel, and occasional tours or entry fees.

- Luxury travelers can spend €200–400+ per day, staying in high-end hotels, dining at top restaurants, and booking private tours, boat charters, or spa treatments.

Prices are generally lower in Montenegro than in Croatia, and significantly lower outside peak season.

The Cost Breakdown

Here's how daily expenses typically shake out:

Accommodation

- Budget: Dorm bed or guesthouse room (€20–40)

- Mid-range: Private hotel room or Airbnb (€60–120)

- Luxury: 4–5 star hotels, villas, boutique stays (€150–400+)

Food & Drink

- Budget: Bakery, street food, fast casual (€10–20)

- Mid-range: Sit-down meals with drinks (€25–50)

- Luxury: Fine dining or tasting menus (€70+)

Transport

- Public buses and ferries are affordable (€5–20 per leg).

- Car rental starts around €30/day, more in summer.

- Taxis and rideshares are pricier—plan ahead to avoid surprises.

Attractions & Activities

- Many of the best things are free: hiking trails, old towns, beaches, and promenades.

- Entry to national parks or major sites ranges from €5–25.

- Guided tours, wine tastings, and excursions vary widely—expect €20–100+ depending on group size and exclusivity.

Seasonal Price Swings

Costs can jump 30–50% in the peak summer months (late June through August). That applies to everything from hotel rooms to car rentals to boat tours. If you're trying to stretch your money, consider the shoulder months (May, early June, September, early October), when prices ease up and the weather is still great.

Where to Save, Where to Splurge

If you're traveling on a tighter budget, it's worth being strategic. A few tips:

- Save on lodging, splurge on experiences. A basic room is fine if you're out all day hiking, swimming, or exploring.

- Eat your big meal at lunch. Many restaurants offer cheaper daytime menus, especially in Croatia.

- Walk or use local transport instead of renting a car if you're sticking to major cities.

- Skip the cruise excursions and book similar activities independently for a fraction of the price.

Budgeting for the Unexpected

Set aside some buffer money. ATM fees, toll roads, last-minute ferry changes, or irresistible wine tastings can throw off even the best-laid budgets. Plan for at least €100–200 extra over your total trip just for peace of mind.

2.2 Choosing Your Travel Style

Traveling in Croatia and Montenegro can be shaped into almost any kind of experience—from barefoot backpacking and scenic train rides to five-star yachts, boutique hotels, and chauffeured wine tours. Understanding what matters most to you (comfort, convenience, spontaneity, privacy) helps you choose a style that keeps your trip fun rather than stressful—or overpriced.

Backpacker Style: Cheap, Flexible, Adventurous

Ideal for solo travelers, students, or anyone looking to stretch their euros and embrace a bit of unpredictability. Backpacking here means shared dorms or simple guesthouses, meals from markets or bakeries, and taking your time with transport.

Croatia's coast is more expensive than the interior, but you can still find hostels and budget-friendly guesthouses in places like Split, Zadar, and even Dubrovnik—if you book ahead. In Montenegro, towns like Kotor and Ulcinj are affordable even in summer, and inland areas like Nikšić or Plav are incredibly cheap and welcoming.

Upsides:

- Maximum freedom and flexibility

- Low daily cost

- Easy to meet other travelers

Downsides:

- Slower transport connections

- Less comfort in summer heat

- Some language and signage barriers in remote areas

Mid-Range Style: Balanced, Comfortable, Independent

This is the sweet spot for many travelers. You get private rooms, good food, and reliable transport—without blowing the budget.

In Croatia, this might mean renting a small apartment in Rovinj, dining at a konoba (tavern), and taking coastal ferries between islands. In Montenegro, you might stay in a villa in Perast, rent a car for day trips, and hike through Durmitor with a local guide.

This style works well for couples, small groups, or families who want a mix of structure and freedom.

Upsides:

- Good comfort for the price
- Wide range of accommodation and dining options
- Easier logistics than strict budget travel

Downsides:

- Can still get pricey in peak season
- May require more advance booking
- Not immune to tourist crowds in popular towns

Luxury Style: Scenic, Private, High-Touch

Luxury travel in this region has matured quickly over the last decade. Croatia especially has leaned into boutique design hotels, wine estates, and Michelin-starred dining. Montenegro's coastline now hosts superyachts, private beach clubs, and spa resorts.

Private sailing trips, wine tastings, historical walking tours with academics—these are all on the menu.

Popular luxury hubs include Dubrovnik, Hvar, Rovinj, and Korčula in Croatia; and Tivat, Sveti Stefan, and the Bay of Kotor in Montenegro.

Upsides:

- Comfort, privacy, and tailored experiences

- Access to high-end dining and private excursions

- Stress-free logistics—many resorts will handle everything

Downsides:

- High cost, especially in summer

- Luxury hubs can feel sanitized or disconnected from local culture

- Limited availability if not booked months in advance

Mixing Travel Styles

You don't have to stick to one approach the whole way through. Many travelers start with mid-range hotels, throw in a splurge for a special night (like a sea-view suite or private boat day), and trim back elsewhere.

- Stay inland or in smaller towns for a few nights to reset your budget.

- Use points or deals to book a nicer hotel in Dubrovnik or Kotor.

- Travel light and invest in unique experiences—a cooking class, a remote mountain hut, a hidden beach only locals use.

This kind of mix-and-match approach keeps your trip dynamic and lets you adapt to changing weather, moods, and discoveries along the way.

2.3 Transportation Options: Flights, Ferries, Buses, Rental Cars

Getting around Croatia and Montenegro is part of the experience—but it's not always straightforward. These countries offer a beautiful but fragmented geography, shaped by mountains, islands, and a coastline full of peninsulas and bays. That means you'll often need to combine different types of transport: ferries, buses, flights, rental cars, and on occasion, a good walk.

Planning your route ahead of time will save you stress and help you use your travel days more efficiently—especially if you're moving between islands or crossing borders.

Flying In and Out

Most international travelers arrive by air. Croatia has several well-connected airports:

- Zagreb (ZAG) – The capital's airport is the busiest in Croatia and the best hub for inland travel.

- Split (SPU) – Ideal for southern Dalmatia and the islands.

- Dubrovnik (DBV) – Good for travelers starting in the far south or crossing to Montenegro.

- Zadar (ZAD) and Pula (PUY) – Serve northern Dalmatia and Istria, often with seasonal flights.

In Montenegro, the two main airports are:

- Podgorica (TGD) – The capital and better for inland Montenegro or the north.

- Tivat (TIV) – Closest to the coast and most convenient if you're headed to Kotor, Budva, or Herceg Novi.

If you're flying into Dubrovnik and planning to cross into Montenegro, keep in mind that public transport is limited and border delays are common. A private transfer or rental car might be worth the money for this leg.

Ferries: Island Hopping and Coastal Cruising

In Croatia, ferries are essential for reaching the islands. The network is robust but not always fast—especially if you're visiting in the shoulder season or aiming to link multiple islands.

Main routes include:

- Split to Hvar, Brač, Vis, and Korčula

- Dubrovnik to Mljet and Korčula (seasonal)

- Rijeka to Cres, Lošinj, and other northern islands

- Zadar to Dugi Otok and nearby islets

There are two main types of ferries:

- Car ferries (slow but reliable, no reservation needed for foot passengers)

- Catamarans (faster, foot passengers only, and often sell out—especially in summer)

Timetables can change depending on the month, so check schedules closely and plan buffer time between connections. Most routes are operated by state-run or regional ferry companies, and tickets are reasonably priced.

Montenegro has far fewer ferry routes. The main one is a short car ferry across the Bay of Kotor (Kamenari–Lepetane), which saves time when driving from Tivat to Herceg Novi. Otherwise, boat trips are mostly for sightseeing rather than practical transport.

Buses: Reliable and Surprisingly Scenic

Both countries have decent long-distance bus networks. They're often the best option for travelers without a car who want to get between cities and towns.

- Croatia: Buses connect most cities and coastal towns, including inland routes to Plitvice Lakes or the Slavonia region. They're usually on time, relatively comfortable, and reasonably priced. Luggage fees are standard (usually a few euros per bag).

- **Montenegro:** Buses are common between Podgorica, Kotor, Budva, and smaller towns, though routes in the mountains can be slow. Some roads are narrow or winding, so patience is required—but the views often make up for it.

Tickets are typically bought at local stations or online. If you're boarding at a station, arrive early, as buses may fill up in summer and signage isn't always clear.

Rental Cars: Freedom and Flexibility

Renting a car opens up areas you simply can't reach by bus or ferry—especially in Montenegro, where public transport is thinner in rural areas and national parks.

Croatia's coastal roads are well-maintained, and driving inland (e.g., to Krka, Plitvice, or Istria's hill towns) is straightforward. Montenegro's roads are more rugged, with tight curves and steep grades in the north. Be cautious if you're not used to mountain driving.

A few things to keep in mind:

- Cross-border fees are common. Always inform the rental company if you plan to cross into Montenegro or Bosnia and Herzegovina.

- Automatic cars are available but limited—book early if you need one.

- Tolls exist on some highways (especially in Croatia). You can pay with euros or cards.

Parking can be a hassle in old towns or beach areas, especially in July and August. Look for lodging that includes parking, or park further out and walk in.

Trains: Limited But Worth Noting

In Croatia, trains are useful mainly for inland routes like Zagreb to Osijek or Rijeka. They're slow and not the best for coastal travel. Montenegro has a notable exception: the scenic train from Bar (on the coast) to Belgrade, which passes through gorges, tunnels, and mountain valleys. If you're headed north toward Serbia, it's a unique ride.

Taxis and Ride Services

Taxis are available in most cities, but prices vary and not all drivers use meters. It's wise to agree on a fare beforehand or use a local ride app when available. In Montenegro, taxis are often cheaper than in Croatia, but quality varies.

Taxis at airports and ferry terminals can charge inflated rates, especially in Dubrovnik. Ask your accommodation to recommend a reliable local driver if you're unsure.

2.4 Apps and Resources for Smart Planning

While the joy of travel often comes from spontaneous discovery, a few smart tools can make planning—and adjusting—your trip much easier. Most travelers find that a mix of digital aids and local advice works best in Croatia and Montenegro, especially given the patchy Wi-Fi and mobile coverage in some rural areas.

This section focuses on types of tools and how to use them effectively—not specific platforms, which can change or become outdated.

Mapping and Navigation

Digital maps are essential, but in certain parts of the Balkans, they're not always precise—especially in mountain areas, older city centers, or hiking trails.

- Offline maps are a lifesaver. Download maps before leaving Wi-Fi zones, particularly for island towns, national parks, and rural roads in Montenegro.

- Use satellite view or street-level images to preview tricky driving areas or remote trailheads.

- Don't rely too heavily on GPS for hiking routes—trail signage is often better in person than on screen, especially in Montenegro's national parks.

In cities like Split, Kotor, or Dubrovnik, maps can help you avoid endless stair climbs or detours through cruise-tour choke points.

Public Transport Schedules

Official websites for bus and ferry companies can be helpful, but they're not always accurate or up to date—especially for local routes.

- Look for apps or local websites that aggregate bus schedules across different operators. Keep in mind that most bus stations are semi-independent and may have different timetables.

- Ferry timetables change seasonally. Always double-check departure points, as some towns (like Split) have multiple docks depending on the route.

- Some apps allow for real-time updates on delays or cancellations, which is handy during stormy weather or in shoulder seasons.

Don't be afraid to ask locals or ticket agents directly—many travelers get more reliable answers from the station office than from online searches.

Currency and Budget Tools

Since both countries use the euro (Montenegro unofficially, Croatia officially since 2023), you don't have to worry about exchanging currency between them—but you still need to track your spending.

- Use budget tracking apps to keep tabs on how much you're spending each day.

- ATM fees vary, so it's worth checking whether your bank offers partner withdrawals abroad.

- Avoid using currency exchange booths in tourist centers—they often charge poor rates.

In smaller towns or on islands, cash is still king. Always carry some euros on you, especially for local buses, small cafes, and roadside shops.

Local Recommendations

No app can replace a good chat with a local host, bartender, or ferry crew member. That said, digital tools can point you in the right direction—especially in areas where tourism is newer and not yet saturated with mainstream guides.

- Look for community-curated recommendations for restaurants, hikes, or swimming spots.

- Keep an eye out for holiday calendars, museum closures, or festival announcements, which may affect opening hours.

- In Montenegro especially, opening hours can shift based on weather, holidays, or even family events—so always call or message ahead when possible.

Language Help

While many Croatians and Montenegrins in tourist areas speak excellent English, a translation app or downloadable phrasebook can be handy in rural areas.

- Pronunciation can be tricky; audio pronunciation tools can help if you're trying to order local dishes or read town signs.

- Download offline translation dictionaries if you're headed to smaller inland villages.

- Basic phrases like "thank you," "please," and "excuse me" go a long way—and are appreciated.

Weather and Conditions

Conditions can change quickly, especially in the mountains or on the coast. Sudden wind shifts (like the bura) can cancel ferries or close roads.

- Use apps with local weather stations for more accurate forecasts.

- Coastal winds and surf conditions are especially important for ferry travel, kayaking, or beach days.

- Montenegro's mountains, even in summer, pack for rapid shifts in temperature or unexpected fog.

Staying Grounded

Even the best apps are tools—not guides. Don't over-plan or try to micromanage every hour. In these countries, the most memorable experiences often come when you follow a local's advice, take a detour off the main path, or linger in a town you hadn't heard of a week ago.

Let tech support your curiosity—not replace it.

Chapter 3: Castles & Capitals — Urban Highlights

Urban life in Croatia and Montenegro isn't flashy or chaotic—it's layered. From the rhythm of Roman ruins in Split to the slow charm of baroque facades in Zagreb, cities in this part of Europe reveal themselves in moments: a street musician under an archway, a grandmother selling figs beside a fortress, a café packed with regulars arguing about football and philosophy in the same breath. This chapter is a guide to some of the most rewarding city stops in both countries, whether you're exploring on foot, cycling past historic gates, or weaving between wine bars and hidden courtyards.

What makes these urban centers special isn't just their landmarks—it's the way history and daily life mix without trying too hard. A palace becomes a neighborhood. A medieval wall becomes a sunset lookout. These cities offer enough depth for slow exploration, but they also work as day trips or launch points. Whether you're chasing architecture, museum visits, or just trying to find the best burek or espresso in town, this section will help you navigate the standout urban hubs with confidence and curiosity.

3.1 Zagreb to Ljubljana Day Trip

Zagreb, Croatia's capital, is one of the most underappreciated capitals in Europe—and maybe that's a good thing. It doesn't try to impress with sweeping skylines or grandiose plazas. Instead, it charms with layers of lived-in beauty: Austro-Hungarian facades, quiet courtyards, and a street culture that thrives on coffee, conversation, and sarcasm. If you spend more than a few hours here, you'll start to feel like a local—or at least understand why locals don't rush through it.

Zagreb's Character: Where Central Europe Meets the Balkans

Zagreb doesn't scream "Mediterranean," and it's not meant to. You won't see the Adriatic here, but you'll feel something else: a central European rhythm tinged with Balkan personality. The city is divided into the historic Upper Town (Gornji Grad) and the livelier Lower Town (Donji Grad), connected by a short but scenic funicular that still runs daily. You can walk both in a day, but it's worth slowing down.

In the Upper Town, you'll find cobblestone streets, medieval towers, and a political heart that still beats beneath the quaint surface—Croatia's parliament sits here, behind St. Mark's Church, known for its tiled rooftop mosaics. A walk through Kamenita Vrata (Stone Gate) leads you into a niche where locals light candles daily, blending civic history with personal ritual.

The Lower Town offers a completely different vibe: wider streets, parks like Zrinjevac, and architecture that reflects the Austro-Hungarian legacy—grand but not sterile. This is also café territory. Take your time. Sit under a canopy. Watch how much of the city seems to operate between sips of espresso.

Museums and Oddities

Zagreb's museum scene mixes the classic with the quirky. The Museum of Broken Relationships is famous for good reason—what started as a personal project turned into a global repository of love and loss. Elsewhere, you'll find collections that speak to the city's broader identity: the Mimara Museum (classic European art), the Croatian Museum of Naïve Art, and the Technical Museum Nikola Tesla, named after the region's most famous inventor.

And don't skip the Dolac Market, especially in the morning. Fresh produce, local cheeses, cured meats, honey, and flower stalls create a sensory map of Croatian daily life. Grab a snack and join the locals at the open-air benches.

Day Tripping to Ljubljana

If you're based in Zagreb for a few days, Ljubljana, the capital of Slovenia, is one of the most rewarding day trips you can take—just under two hours away by train or car. The city is small, walkable, and effortlessly elegant without feeling pretentious. Its baroque architecture, leafy riverbanks, and vibrant student scene make it feel almost storybook-like.

Cross the Dragon Bridge, meander through the Central Market, or ride the funicular up to Ljubljana Castle for panoramic views. It's easy to get around, most locals speak English well, and the food scene balances Slavic heartiness with Italian flair.

One tip: try to avoid weekends if you want to miss the bigger crowds and enjoy a slower local pace. Trains run regularly, but early morning departures give you a full day in the city. Alternatively, renting a car gives you the option to visit Lake Bled or Postojna Cave on the way.

Zagreb Practical Notes

- Transit: Trams are efficient and cheap; the city center is walkable.

- Seasons: Spring and autumn offer the best mix of weather and activity. Winters can be cold but cozy—especially around Advent, when the Christmas markets are among the best in the region.

- Costs: Zagreb is cheaper than most European capitals. Coffee is around €1.50–2.00, and a decent meal can cost €10–15.

3.2 Split: Diocletian's Palace & Seaside Vibes

Split is a city that grew inside a Roman emperor's retirement plan—and never left. Diocletian's Palace isn't just a historical site; it's the center of the city. People live, shop, and eat in its stone corridors. Laundry hangs between 1,700-year-old columns. Musicians play under vaulted arches where soldiers once marched. This blend of ancient bones and modern soul is what makes Split compelling—not just its beauty, but its authenticity.

The Heartbeat of Diocletian's Palace

Unlike ruins set apart from modern life, Split's palace is a living, breathing organism. It's technically a UNESCO World Heritage Site, but don't expect velvet ropes and hushed tones. Here, cafés spill out into the Peristyle, teenagers ride bikes through alleyways that date back to Roman times, and you might find a wine bar tucked under a former temple.

The palace complex includes the Cathedral of St. Domnius, originally Diocletian's mausoleum. Its bell tower offers one of the best views in Split—climb it near sunset for a sweeping look over red rooftops and the Adriatic beyond. Just across from the cathedral is the Temple of Jupiter, now a baptistery. The Egyptian sphinxes brought here by Diocletian are still lounging nearby, watching over the city.

Riva, Beaches, and Daily Rhythm

Beyond the palace, Riva, the waterfront promenade, is where Split unwinds. Locals stroll arm in arm, kids eat gelato, and every café table seems perfectly angled toward the sea. Mornings are quiet, ideal for a walk or bike ride; by evening, it hums with conversation and live music.

If you're staying more than a day, make time for a swim. Bačvice Beach is a sandy, shallow spot just 10 minutes from the center—great for people-watching and joining a game of picigin, a local ball game played in shallow water. Kasjuni Beach and Kašjuni Cove, set below Marjan Hill, are quieter, with pebbles, pine trees, and calmer water.

Markets and Everyday Life

Split's Green Market (Pazar), just east of the palace walls, is a great place to stock up on fruit, cheese, dried figs, or olives if you're self-catering—or just hungry. Early mornings are best, when produce is fresh and the crowds thinner.

Next to the bus station, the Fish Market (Peškarija) is another sensory dive into local life. Here, the scent of salt and sardines fills the air, and negotiations are fast and loud. Even if you're not cooking, it's worth a look just to see what caught the Adriatic overnight.

Hiking, Viewpoints, and Detours

For a break from city streets, walk or bike up Marjan Hill. It's an easy ascent and rewards you with sweeping views over Split's harbor and the nearby islands. There are chapels, shaded paths, and great spots for a picnic.

If you have more time, Split also makes a great base for day trips—to Trogir, Klis Fortress, or the islands of Brač, Šolta, and Hvar, each reachable by ferry or catamaran.

Split Practical Notes

- **Transit:** The old town is pedestrian-only. Ferries and buses leave from terminals next to the harbor.

- **Seasons:** Late spring and early fall are best. July and August bring intense heat and crowds.

- **Costs:** Slightly more expensive than inland cities. Expect €15–20 for a meal, but bakeries and markets offer cheaper eats.

3.3 Dubrovnik's City Walls & Storytelling Heritage

Dubrovnik is many things at once: a walled fortress city rising from limestone cliffs, a UNESCO World Heritage Site, a modern-day magnet for film crews and cruise ships, and a place where history clings to every alley. But beyond its famous looks, Dubrovnik is a deeply layered city—part museum, part stage, part home. The locals who still live within the walls are custodians of centuries of resilience and reinvention. If you listen closely—to a guide, a waiter, a grandmother stringing laundry from her stone window—you'll hear the same message over and over: Dubrovnik was never meant to be conquered easily.

Even seasoned travelers sometimes mistake Dubrovnik for a place you "do" in a day or two. And while you can technically tick off its major sights in 48 hours, that's not really the point. To understand this city, you need to look beyond the surface polish—beyond the tour groups and ice cream stands—and give yourself the time to absorb its atmosphere. This is a place where geography, history, and local pride intersect with intense beauty. It deserves attention not just for what you see, but for what it has endured and become.

The Walls That Shaped a City

The city walls of Dubrovnik are more than just architecture—they're an unbroken loop of stone storytelling. Encircling the Old Town for nearly two kilometers, with forts and towers rising at strategic points, the walls were never breached by a hostile army. They were built and rebuilt over centuries, adapting to changing threats, from Ottoman invasions to the encroachment of the sea. Walk them end to end, and you walk through 800 years of military strategy, civic pride, and stubborn independence.

The walk itself takes about 90 minutes if you're steady and don't stop much, but few visitors can resist lingering. The views are consistently stunning: terracotta rooftops below, the deep blue Adriatic to one side, and the looming mass of Mount Srđ behind the city. There's no shade, so bring water and wear a hat, especially in summer. The light here can be fierce—and beautiful. Early morning or late afternoon are the best times to avoid crowds and catch the softest light for photography.

Each section of the wall offers something different. The Minčeta Tower, on the northwest corner, is the highest point and offers the best panorama. On the seaward side, the St. John Fortress guards the old port, and from the Bokar Fortress, you can look down toward Fort Lovrijenac, the city's dramatic outpost perched on a separate cliff. These aren't just defensive relics—they're symbols of a city that always protected itself, diplomatically and architecturally.

Old Town: Living Layers of Time

Inside the walls, Dubrovnik's Old Town is a tight-knit grid of limestone streets polished smooth by centuries of foot traffic. The central street, Stradun, runs from Pile Gate to the Old Port, and it's always bustling. But step just one alley off the main route and the volume drops. Suddenly you're in a shaded stone corridor, laundry overhead, a cat napping on a windowsill, a chipped religious icon in a wall niche. These side streets reveal the everyday Dubrovnik—the city that still lives and breathes behind the tourism façade.

The Rector's Palace, once the seat of power in the Republic of Ragusa (Dubrovnik's former identity), blends Gothic, Renaissance, and Baroque elements. It now houses a cultural history museum that helps piece together how this once-independent republic managed to maintain neutrality and prosperity between much larger powers. Dubrovnik's merchants were renowned for their diplomacy and skill at staying out of others' wars. That spirit is still part of the city's self-image.

Nearby, the Franciscan Monastery hosts one of the oldest pharmacies in Europe, which has operated continuously since 1317. The pharmacy is still functioning—though part of it is now a museum—and gives a rare, tangible link to everyday life in the medieval city. It's not just about big historical moments here; it's about continuity and survival.

War, Reconstruction, and Local Memory

For all its visual perfection, Dubrovnik carries scars. During the Croatian War of Independence in the early 1990s, the city was shelled for months despite its UNESCO status and historical significance. Nearly 70% of buildings in the Old Town were damaged. Many visitors don't realize that the rooftops they admire—those bright, unweathered tiles—are part of that rebuilding. The older, darker tiles survived; the new ones mark where destruction happened.

The War Photo Limited gallery, just a few steps off Stradun, offers a stark counterpoint to the romanticized image of Dubrovnik. Its exhibitions document the conflicts of the Balkans and beyond through the lens of photojournalism. It's not an easy space, but it's essential. Dubrovnik doesn't hide its traumas; it integrates them, turning them into stories worth hearing.

And stories are everywhere. Ask a local about the siege. About the earthquake of 1667. About the old days before Game of Thrones made the city globally famous. Many will tell you about how the crowds have changed their city—but they'll also say it's still theirs, and that matters.

Escape the Crowds (Without Leaving the City)

Dubrovnik can be crowded—especially from June to September, when cruise ships anchor daily and the Old Town fills by 10 a.m. But there are ways to breathe.

Climb early: Be at the walls when they open. You'll have space, peace, and cooler temperatures.

Get lost deliberately: Wander the backstreets north of Stradun or climb the long, quiet staircases toward Buža Bar, a cliffside café perched just outside the walls where you can swim straight from the rocks into the sea.

Explore at night: After sunset, the cruise crowds thin, lights glow on the old stones, and the city becomes softer, quieter—more itself.

Cable Car to Mount Srđ

For a full view of the city and coastline, take the Dubrovnik Cable Car up to Mount Srđ. On a clear day, you'll see the old city, the sea, and the nearby Elaphiti Islands. The top also holds Fort Imperial, built during the Napoleonic Wars and later used as a defensive post in the 1990s conflict. There's a museum inside covering the siege and Dubrovnik's defense.

Alternatively, you can hike up the mountain—it's about an hour on a marked trail that begins near the city. Steep but doable, and rewarding in every way.

Beyond the Walls: Day Trips and Detours

Dubrovnik makes a solid base for exploring the southern Dalmatian coast, and even slipping into Montenegro. But within Croatia, don't miss:

- Lokrum Island, just a 10-minute ferry ride from the Old Port. It's a nature reserve with peacocks, botanical gardens, ruins, and a peaceful swimming spot at the Dead Sea lagoon.

- Cavtat, a charming seaside town 30 minutes south. Smaller, quieter, and full of good seafood, it's where some locals actually prefer to live.

- Trsteno Arboretum, a few kilometers north, with ancient trees, sea views, and Renaissance gardens—less visited, very atmospheric.

Dubrovnik Practical Notes

- When to Go: April to early June and September to October offer the best balance of good weather and manageable crowds. Winter is beautiful but quieter, with fewer ferries and limited hours at some attractions.

- Getting There: Dubrovnik Airport (DBV) is 30–40 minutes from town. Buses meet most flights. No train service connects to Dubrovnik, but long-distance buses are reliable and scenic.

- Getting Around: The Old Town is pedestrian-only. Everything within the walls is walkable. Ferries depart from the Old Port and Gruž Harbor.

- Costs: Dubrovnik is one of the pricier spots in Croatia. Expect €20–30 for a sit-down dinner, and around €30 for wall access. Budget accordingly, but you'll get value in views and atmosphere.

3.4 Kotor & the Bay of Kotor Towns

Tucked into a horseshoe-shaped bay and surrounded by steep limestone cliffs, Kotor doesn't reveal itself all at once. It's a place that appears slowly—first as a cluster of medieval rooftops glimpsed from a winding coastal road, then as a walled Old Town that feels improbably well-preserved. Kotor doesn't clamor for attention. It draws you in with shadows, stone, and silence.

The Bay of Kotor is often called Europe's southernmost fjord, though geologically it's a ria—a drowned river valley. Either way, the setting is dramatic. Towns like Perast, Herceg Novi, and Tivat curve around the bay's edge like a chain of pearls, each with its own story. The mountains rise almost straight from the sea, and the roads cling to the shore in narrow, looping ribbons. Ferries, sailboats, and kayaks glide between islets. Church towers rise above orange-tiled roofs. There are few places in Europe where water and stone meet in such quiet harmony.

Unlike Dubrovnik, Kotor feels less manicured. It's still lived-in, still rough in places. Cats sleep in the sun against walls older than most nations. Laundry hangs beside carved lintels. There's beauty, but not perfection—and that's part of the charm.

Inside Kotor's Walls: A City Shaped by Empires

Kotor's Old Town, a UNESCO World Heritage Site, is a maze of narrow alleys, vaulted archways, and secret courtyards. The layout is compact—less than half a square kilometer—but dense with history. You'll find Romanesque churches, Venetian palaces, Austrian fortifications, and Ottoman echoes. Empires came and went, but Kotor absorbed each one and kept moving.

Start your visit at Sea Gate, the main entrance built in 1555 during Venetian rule. Just inside is the main square, Trg od Oružja (Armory Square), where cafés spill into the open and the Clock Tower has kept time since the 17th century. From there, wander at will. The town is small enough that you won't get lost for long.

One of the most notable landmarks is St. Tryphon's Cathedral, dating to 1166. It was damaged by earthquakes and rebuilt multiple times, but the carved stone façade and relics of Kotor's patron saint still draw visitors. Inside, look up: the wooden ceiling is an artwork in itself.

Other highlights include the Church of St. Nicholas, an Orthodox anchor in a mostly Catholic town; and the Maritime Museum, which tells the story of Kotor's long naval tradition. This was once a city of sailors and merchants, and its residents were known across the Adriatic.

Unlike many historic towns, Kotor hasn't scrubbed away its rough edges. Look closely and you'll see faded murals, cracked plaster, and stray cats lounging under chipped icons. There's no over-restoration here. The city wears its age honestly.

Hiking the Fortress Walls Above Kotor

For many, the defining experience in Kotor is the hike to San Giovanni Fortress, which towers high above the town on a steep slope of scrub and stone. The climb is no joke: over 1,300 steps with little shade, uneven footing, and no water stops. But if you're up for the challenge, the reward is massive.

Start early—ideally before 8 a.m.—to beat both the heat and the crowds. The entrance is near the northern gate of the Old Town, and there's a modest fee to access the trail. The views get better with every step. You'll see the red roofs of Kotor spread below, the bay curling into the mountains like a mirror, and clouds drifting low over the peaks.

Halfway up, you'll pass the Church of Our Lady of Remedy, built in the 16th century during a plague outbreak. The trail narrows and steepens from there, with stone walls hugging the switchbacks. At the top, the crumbling fortress of San Giovanni (St. John) waits. Built and modified over centuries—by Byzantines, Venetians, Austrians—it's not so much a monument as a memory of resistance. Sit on the edge, feel the wind, and you'll understand why people fought so hard for this place.

You can descend the way you came, or take an alternate ladder route through the old grazing lands beyond the walls, looping back through olive groves and local gardens. It's longer, but quieter, and gives you a glimpse of rural life just beyond the tourist zone.

Perast: The Bay's Sleeping Beauty

About 20 minutes north of Kotor, the town of Perast is impossibly picturesque. It has just one main street along the waterfront and only a few hundred residents, but 19 baroque palaces and 16 churches. Perast feels like a film set, frozen in time.

No cars are allowed in the town center, so you'll hear mostly footfalls, waves, and church bells. Take a slow walk along the promenade, stop for a coffee or a seafood lunch, and admire the offshore islands—Our Lady of the Rocks and St. George—each with its own story. You can hire a small boat for a short ride to the islands; Our Lady of the Rocks is manmade, built on centuries of sunken ships and rocks dropped by fishermen, who still hold an annual "Fašinada" ceremony to maintain the tradition.

Perast is best in the early morning or late evening, when the day-trippers have gone and the town feels like it belongs to the bay again.

Tivat, Herceg Novi, and Hidden Corners

Tivat, just around the bend from Kotor, is often dismissed as the modern sibling—but it's worth a look. Once a sleepy naval base, it's now home to Porto Montenegro, a sleek marina filled with superyachts. There are beach clubs, boutiques, and fusion restaurants here, catering to a different kind of visitor. Some will find it polished to a fault; others will welcome the contrast.

Herceg Novi, closer to the mouth of the bay, has a more lived-in feel. It's a town of stairs—literally hundreds of them—linking the Old Town to seaside promenades and fortress ruins. The Kanli Kula Fortress offers panoramic views, and the Savina Monastery, just outside town, is a serene stop with ancient trees and a rich Orthodox tradition.

There are also lesser-known villages like Prčanj, Dobrota, and Risan—places where the rhythm slows even more. Here, you'll find stone houses with painted shutters, quiet waterfront cafés, and swimming spots known only to locals. Rent a bike or kayak and explore at your own pace. The bay rewards slowness.

Bay Travel Tips

- Getting Around: Local buses run regularly between towns. Boats and water taxis are also available and often faster. Some visitors rent scooters or small cars, but roads are narrow and often crowded.

- Where to Stay: Kotor has the most variety, from boutique hotels inside the Old Town to quiet guesthouses in Dobrota. Perast is romantic but limited in options. Tivat caters more to luxury travelers.

- When to Visit: May, June, and September offer the best balance of weather and calm. July and August bring more tourists, especially cruise ship crowds in Kotor.

- **Language and Culture:** Montenegrins are warm, proud, and multilingual. A few words of Montenegrin (or Serbian) go a long way: *hvala* (thank you), *dobar dan* (good day), *izvinite* (excuse me).

Chapter 4 – Islands & Coastal Routes

The Adriatic coast of Croatia and Montenegro isn't just about beautiful beaches and scenic waterfronts—it's also a natural playground for island-hopping, road trips, and seaside wandering. The islands scattered off the Dalmatian coast offer their own distinct personalities, from party scenes to medieval calm, olive groves to lavender fields. In Montenegro, while fewer in number, the coastal hideaways are just as captivating—places where pine forests meet cliffs that plunge into the sea.

This chapter is your guide to getting out on the water or hitting the open road. Whether you're piecing together an island-to-island journey or planning a scenic drive with sea views at every turn, this section gives you the practical info to make it smooth—and the cultural detail to make it meaningful. From ferry routes to hidden beaches, local quirks to seasonal tips, it's all about traveling with intention and curiosity.

4.1 Island-Hopping Basics: Ferry Logistics

Island-hopping in Croatia is not only possible—it's one of the best ways to experience the Adriatic. The country has over 1,200 islands, though only about 50 are inhabited. The most visited lie in the central and southern Dalmatian archipelago—close to cities like Split, Dubrovnik, and Zadar. Ferry routes crisscross this region, forming a loose network that allows you to move between islands with relative ease, especially in summer. But "ease" comes with a few caveats.

Planning ferry travel here takes a little patience. Schedules vary by season, routes aren't always daily, and not every island connects directly to the next. Think of the ferry system as a web with a few main hubs—Split, Dubrovnik, Zadar, and Šibenik—from which smaller spokes fan out to individual islands. Most travelers begin and end their trips in these mainland cities.

The Big Picture: How the Ferry System Works

There are two main types of ferries you'll use: car ferries (slower, larger, cheaper) and catamarans (passenger-only, faster, and often more scenic). Car ferries are ideal if you're renting a vehicle and want to bring it island to island, though parking and road infrastructure vary wildly from one island to another. On some smaller islands, a car can be more hassle than it's worth.

Catamarans are best for travelers moving light and fast. They connect major islands like Hvar, Brač, and Korčula with the mainland and, in some cases, each other. During peak summer months (June to September), they run several times a day. Off-season, things slow down considerably—some routes drop to once daily or disappear entirely.

When planning, always double-check seasonal schedules. A route that looks perfect in August may not run at all in April or October. The majority of routes are point-to-point, meaning they're designed to take you to one island, not between multiple. For multi-island journeys, you often have to loop back to the mainland first. This isn't as inefficient as it sounds—it can actually give you time to explore another city before hopping back out to sea.

Mainland Ports That Matter

- Split is the busiest ferry port in Croatia and the most practical launch point for island travel. From here, you can reach Brač (via Supetar), Hvar (Stari Grad or Hvar Town), Šolta, Vis, and Korčula. It's the most flexible base for planning complex itineraries.

- Dubrovnik, though better known for its Old Town, also offers routes to islands like Mljet, Korčula, and Šipan. However, connections are more limited than from Split.

- Zadar and Šibenik serve the northern and central Dalmatian islands like Ugljan, Dugi Otok, and Žirje—less touristy but just as rewarding.

- In Montenegro, ferry travel is limited to short routes—such as the quick hop across the Bay of Kotor between Kamenari and Lepetane. Montenegro's coastline is better suited to road trips, private boats, or occasional charter cruises.

Buying Tickets & Boarding: Practical Tips

Tickets for major ferry routes can be bought in person at port kiosks or booked online ahead of time, which is wise during the busy season. For car ferries, showing up early is essential—even with a ticket, boarding is first come, first served, especially in high summer when cars line up hours in advance.

Catamarans have assigned seating on most routes, and your ticket reserves a specific spot. That said, don't count on it being quiet—popular journeys (like Split to Hvar in July) often feel like rush hour with sea views. Bring water, sun protection, and patience.

Baggage rules are relaxed on most ferries, but catamarans may ask you to stow larger bags in dedicated racks near the entrance. Keep essentials on hand. If you're traveling with bikes, double-check which routes allow them—policies vary by line and vessel.

Island Transfers: Making the Most of Your Route

Let's say you're planning a trip across Brač, Hvar, and Korčula—a popular combination. Start in Split, take the car ferry to Supetar (Brač), then either return to Split and catch a catamaran to Hvar or head to Bol on the south side of Brač, which sometimes connects directly to Jelsa on Hvar via seasonal catamaran.

From Hvar Town, you can find a fast catamaran to Korčula, especially during summer. From Korčula, ferries head to both Dubrovnik and back to Split, so you can loop your route depending on where you fly in or out.

This type of journey takes planning, but if you sync the timetables right, it's smooth. And when things don't line up perfectly? That's the Adriatic invitation to slow down, spend an extra night, and let the rhythm of island life take over.

Off-Season Considerations

If you're traveling in the shoulder months (April–May or late September–October), ferries still run, but with reduced frequency. Lodging is easier to find, prices drop, and towns are quieter. But that also means fewer backup options if you miss a boat or need to change plans.

In the dead of winter, only the most essential routes operate—mostly for locals. Some hotels, restaurants, and bus services shut down entirely. That said, visiting in winter can be deeply rewarding if you're prepared. You'll meet fewer tourists and more residents, see real daily life, and experience the stark beauty of the islands without filters.

Local Ferry Culture

Ferries aren't just tourist vessels—they're part of local life. You'll see schoolkids commuting, delivery vans onboard, and elderly residents carrying baskets of vegetables from the mainland. Don't expect luxury or frills. Do expect a kind of Mediterranean pragmatism: slow, steady, and largely indifferent to your timetable. That's part of the charm.

On deck, locals head straight to the shady side. Tourists crowd the railings for photos. The sound of water slapping the hull, the scent of engine oil, and the clang of chains at the dock all become part of the rhythm of island travel.

4.2 Hvar, Korčula & Brač Highlights

What Makes These Islands Special

Hvar, Korčula, and Brač are among the Adriatic's most beloved islands—but each offers a distinctly different flavor. Hvar pulses with nightlife and history; Korčula mixes fortified charm with grape-infused calm; Brač balances outdoor adventure with traditional villages and beaches. Together, they make an ideal island-hopping trio that reflects the diversity of Dalmatian life.

Hvar: Lavender Fields, Wine, and Sun-Drenched Evenings

Town Life and Architecture

Hvar Town, on the island's north coast, starts to feel alive as the catamaran approaches at dawn. Its golden stone walls glow in the morning light, framed by towering Adriatic pines. Once disembarked, you're drawn toward the vast Pjaca (main square), bordered by cafés—some a century old, others set in medieval vaults. A climb up to the Fortica or Španjola Fortress, built in the 16th century, rewards with sweeping views over lavender fields, Pakleni Islands, and distant Pelješac.

The streets are perfect for aimless wandering, revealing Gothic palaces, neoclassical churches, and hidden courtyards. Stop in at St. Stephen's Cathedral, in the heart of town. Inside you'll find ornate chapels and resin-scented candles left by pilgrims drawn to its relics. The architecture here reflects Hvar's past as a Venetian seafaring hub—elegant, sunwashed stone with carved details that have mirrored sunlight for centuries.

Lavender, Wine, and Local Flavor

If you time your visit in June or July, lavender fields on the hill above town perfume the air. A short drive brings you to one of several small lavender farms where you can see distillation in action—and buy handcrafted oils or soaps directly from producers.

Nearby vineyards produce Plavac Mali, a dark-skinned red grape coaxed into life by rocky soil and relentless sun. Many local wineries offer walks through vines and tastings on shaded terraces—perfect for long conversations between sips.

Beach Life and Island Hopping

Beach culture in Hvar is varied. Pokonji Dol is close to town but a little rocky. Take a short stroll out the harbor and you'll find Zaraće Cove, where children swim off rocks and couples sunbathe under pine trees. For more seclusion, consider a day trip to the Pakleni Islands, which are five minutes away by taxi boat. Here, you can swim in hidden coves, paddle quietly, and stop for beachside seafood platters.

Nightlife is Hvar stripped to its essence: clubs, bars, restaurants with a typically Mediterranean late-night atmosphere. Start early with wine or cocktails in a wine bar; move on to pizza in the square, then live music in tucked-away gardens or clubs. But there's an edge of local authenticity—you're more likely to strike up a conversation with a fisherman at dusk than in a pre-planned tourist venue.

Korčula: "Little Dubrovnik" with Wine Under Vine-Laced Arches

Historic Center and Old-World Roots

Korčula Town, often called "Little Dubrovnik," is encircled by medieval walls and fortified towers. Unlike Dubrovnik, it's smaller—intimate. The streets are arranged in a fishbone pattern, designed to slow sea breezes and diffuse sunlight. As you wander, you'll find baroque homes, small palaces, hidden piazzas, and Gothic churches—all in golden stone.

The Cathedral of St. Mark, with its bell tower, offers views over terra-cotta roofs and surrounding Kornati islets. Near the waterfront, fishermen repair nets and locals gather over coffee or rakija-soaked conversation.

Taste of Tradition

Korčula is home to one of Croatia's red wines—Grk, grown only on the Pelješac peninsula and nearby Korčula's dry hills. White wine lovers shouldn't miss Rukatac (also known as Pošip), a dry, vivid white grape cultivated in the Stari Grad plain. Wineries here are family-run, and tastings often happen on terraces overlooking vineyards and sea.

Local dishes lean into fresh ingredients. Brudet, a fish stew, is common in winter; in summer you'll find gelato in multiple flavors—fig, lavender, lemon—served near the main square. There are also wood-fired breads, small pastries, and seafood platters at seaside konobas.

Beaches, Bocce, and Quiet Evenings

Beaches near Korčula Town cluster on the Ljubač shoreline and Pupnatska Luka. Both are pebble-and-sand spots with clear water and pine shade. Locals love bocce courts beside the sea, and you'll often find friendly matches going early or late in the day.

Evenings in Korčula are serene. After dinner, wander the water's edge. Small lanterns glow on the rippling sea. A cappuccino or glass of wine is rarely rushed.

Brač: Outdoor Spirit and Island Heartbeat

Supetar and Bol: Village Life and Landscape

Supetar, Brač's main ferry port, is a good base for exploring the island's interior. It's a village where bike stands share space with fishing boats, and each café spills local energy onto the waterfront.

Bol, on the southern coast, is home to Zlatni Rat (Golden Horn), one of the Adriatic's most distinctive beaches—thin, shifting, peninsula-like, and popular with windsurfers. The day often begins with surfers riding morning breezes, and ends with families strolling along the palm-lined waterfront.

Mountains, Olive Groves, and Village Exploration

Brač isn't just about beaches—it's also alpine in places. Vidova Gora, the island's highest peak at nearly 780 m, offers hiking routes with far-reaching panoramas that include Hvar, Korčula, and distant Pelješac.

Drive or bike lanes through hills dotted with olive trees and stone walls. Small villages like Pucisca, known for stone-cutting tradition, have limestone houses and artisanal workshops. The town's schools still train new generations in hand-carved stone.

Culture, Food, and Peaceful Hidden Spots

Experience Brač on a slow day: wander lanes where sunlight slants through cypress trees, settle at a konoba with olive salad (fresh oil and capers) and grilled fish, then walk out to a headland for sunset—sometimes you'll share the moment with only a few other observers.

Island-Hopping Itinerary Tips

For those visiting all three islands:

- Base in Split, with returns each night. Ideal for limited time, but less immersive.

- Split → Brač (Supetar) overnight, then Bol for a day, then Bol → Hvar, overnight, followed by Hvar → Korčula, and back to Split or Dubrovnik depending on flight plans.

- Pad variability: seasonal catamarans connect islands directly in summer but slow down off-season.

Even two nights per island allows a good sense of its rhythm—each island plays to a different tune.

4.3 Montenegro's Hidden Coastal Gems: Perast & Sveti Stefan

Montenegro's coastline is shorter, steeper, and more dramatic than Croatia's. Instead of many islands, there are fewer, but more dramatic peninsulas and islets like the legendary Sveti Stefan—a medieval village-turned-luxury resort. Then there's Perast, which in its quiet, marble-and-gothic stillness, feels like a living fossil. These gems offer a contrast to Montenegro's more known seaside towns, giving travelers access to near-mythic beauty and serenity.

Perast: Where Still Water and Stone Meet

A Glimpse of Old Maritime Grandeur

Perast, north of Kotor, is an 18th-century Venetian jewel. The grand stone villas face the sea, their windows reflecting off still water. Walk along the single main street and you'll feel suspended in time—side-by-side with fishermen, artists, and tourists who are there to drink it in.

The Our Lady of the Rocks islet, accessible by boat or water taxi, is essential. The small church and its painted ceilings sit atop a man-made island of stones dropped by sailors over centuries. Later, St. George's

Island, a natural islet with a crumbling Benedictine monastery, looms next door.

Morning and Evening: Quiet Magic

Perast is best before 9 a.m. or after dusk. Days are for day trippers; evenings are for locals. Start your day with black coffee at a harbor café—watch the water catch light. Leave for a boat ride, return before the lunch crowd, and end with dinner in a centuries-old hall with wooden beams and stone arches.

Sveti Stefan: Iconic Island Village

A Landmark of Contrast

Sveti Stefan is a tiny island (connected to mainland by a narrow land bridge) made of coral-hued stone houses and tile-roofed alleyways. It once housed a fishing community; now it's a luxury resort with villas, fine dining, and gated exclusivity. The juxtaposition can be jarring—being offered a meal in a 15th-century house at €100-per-plate standards, surrounded by private beaches and polished concierge services.

The resort understandably limits access, but you can still walk around the causeway and admire it from nearby public beaches—especially from the pebbled sandy shores below Hotel Maestral or the newer Sveti Stefan Beach Resort. Here you get the fantasy without the price, with excellent seaside restaurants and occasional access to resort services like spa menus or private dinner events.

Local Access and Cultural Notes

Many Montenegrins come for half-day visits to dine or lounge—even if they won't stay overnight in the resort. Traditional fooders like kačamak and priganice are on offer at nearby villages. Take a short drive inland to the village of Pržna or Radanovići for more local dining, craft shops, and olive groves.

How to Visit These Gems

- By car: Both towns are along the main coastal road. Parking can be tricky—plan to park a bit away and walk.

- By boat: Many day cruises around the bay stop at Perast or near Sveti Stefan—for the best light, look for sunset options departing from Kotor or Budva.

- By water taxi: Faster and more personal than cruises; negotiable by price and route.

Best Times, Practical Notes

- Timing: Early morning and late afternoon are quieter and offer better light for photos. Perast is serene in May–June or September–October—less traffic, more wind in your hair.

- Open access: Perast is open to all. Sveti Stefan island isn't—unless you're a guest. But the causeway and nearby viewpoints are freely accessible.

- Dining: Expect symmetrical old buildings with stone patios and white linens. There's an entry fee into the resort for non-staying guests during peak season—but often with a drink or appetizer included.

Together, these sections give you more than just a list of stops. They help you feel the personality of each place—its textures, modes, and pace.

4.4 Scenic Drives & Coastal Walks

In both Croatia and Montenegro, some of the most memorable moments happen between the major sights—on winding coastal roads, clifftop viewpoints, shaded promenades, and footpaths that hug the sea. This is where the countries reveal their rhythm: where light glints off the water at just the right angle, or where you stumble upon a sleepy fishing village you hadn't planned to visit. In this section, we'll cover both scenic drives and coastal walks that offer atmosphere, history, and a sense of place—ideal for travelers who prefer to wander with their eyes open.

The Dalmatian Coast by Car: Twisting Roads and Breathtaking Views

Driving the Croatian coast, especially the stretch between Split and Dubrovnik, is not just about getting from point A to B. It's about everything in between. This coastal road—part of the D8, also known as the Jadranska Magistrala—is a two-lane highway that winds its way through villages, vineyards, cliffside pine forests, and towns perched above bright blue water.

You'll pass olive groves, old Austro-Hungarian tunnels, roadside stands selling fresh figs and lavender, and dramatic coastal drop-offs. There are dozens of places to pull over: for coffee in a sleepy harbor, a swim off a quiet cove, or just to breathe in the Adriatic air. It's not the kind of road where you blast through in a hurry. Most people average 40–50 km/h when factoring in curves and stops. And that's a good thing.

Best scenic stretch: The section between Makarska and Ploče, where the Biokovo mountains rise steeply on one side and the Adriatic opens wide on the other, is one of the most beautiful drives in Europe. Sunset here is particularly striking, with golden light catching on limestone ridges and old church spires.

Off-the-path detour: Take a detour up into the Biokovo Skywalk near Podgora. You'll drive a narrow, steep road up the mountain to a glass platform at 1,228 meters with views stretching as far as Italy on a clear day. This route isn't for nervous drivers—but it's unforgettable.

Montenegro's Coastal Ribbons

Montenegro's coast, though much shorter, is no less dramatic. If anything, the elevation shifts are sharper and the scenery more condensed. The most striking drive is the one that loops around the Bay of Kotor (Boka Kotorska), where mountains plunge into fjord-like water.

Start in Kotor and take the road that hugs the shoreline toward Perast. From here, the road narrows—stone houses and jetties come right up to the asphalt. Locals hang laundry or unload fishing nets just feet from passing cars. There's a sense that time is layered here, like the sea and the mountains have been in conversation for centuries and you've just arrived mid-sentence.

Loop option: From Kotor, you can loop through Risan, head up the serpentines (the Kotor-Lovćen road, with 25 switchbacks), and emerge high above the bay. The view from the Njeguši Pass is staggering—a deep blue basin surrounded by jagged peaks and scattered white buildings. It's a route best done early in the day, especially in summer when heat and traffic pick up.

Tips for driving in both countries:

- Roads are narrow and require focus, especially near blind curves. Locals often drive fast—hold your line and don't panic.

- Fuel stations can be sparse in rural areas, so fill up before detouring inland.

- Pay attention to signage: "Privatna cesta" means private road; "Zabranjen prolaz" means no access.

- Always keep coins for tolls and parking meters—many small villages still operate with cash-only machines.

Walking the Promenades: Seaside Routes With Soul

If driving brings you to these towns, walking helps you experience them. From palm-lined coastal promenades to cliffside trails, walking is how locals and visitors alike slow the pulse and connect to their surroundings.

Split's Riva & Marjan Park

The Riva promenade in Split is the city's social lung. Stretching along the waterfront just outside Diocletian's Palace, it's where locals gather at sunset, children scoot along the wide marble path, and tourists pause over coffee or gelato. It's not a long walk—barely half a kilometer—but it's packed with atmosphere.

For a more immersive stroll, walk west from the Riva to Marjan Hill. The trail starts with steps that climb up to Vidilica Café, a panoramic viewpoint, and then snakes through pine forests, hidden chapels, and quiet benches. The entire loop is around 7–8 km and gives you sweeping views of the city and surrounding islands.

Dubrovnik's Coastal Paths

Everyone knows the city walls walk—yes, it's iconic, and yes, it's worth doing, especially early morning before the heat and crowds set in. But there are other, lesser-known walks that reveal just as much beauty.

One favorite is the path from Pile Gate to Lapad, following the coastal edge past

Boninovo cliffs and local swimming holes. You'll pass graffiti-tagged rock ledges where teenagers dive into the sea, old staircases leading to no-name coves, and views of the open Adriatic. Locals walk dogs here or swim in the late afternoon. Tourists rarely wander this far from the Old Town.

Kotor's City Walls & Ladder of Kotor

In Montenegro, Kotor's walls and the Ladder of Kotor offer a stunning vertical walk. The official stairs wind up to the San Giovanni Fortress, offering unmatched views over the bay. But for a more rustic and less crowded experience, try the old Austro-Hungarian switchbacks just behind the city. The "ladder" leads to a shepherd's hut, a small stone chapel, and eventually connects to trails leading deep into Lovćen National Park.

Bring sturdy shoes, water, and patience—the climb is no joke. But the views, especially with early morning fog over the bay or golden afternoon light, are worth every step.

Sveti Stefan to Budva Promenade

This walk is short but postcard-perfect. Starting from the public beach near Sveti Stefan, follow the paved seaside path north toward Pržno and then Budva. You'll walk through olive groves, shaded coastal parks, and past rocky inlets. Locals stop to swim off rocks; fishermen cast lines from quiet points; families picnic in pine-shaded coves.

This trail is best enjoyed in the early morning or late evening. The golden-hour light, the gentle surf, and the calm pace make it an ideal bookend to a full day of sightseeing.

Final Notes: Planning for the Journey Itself

- Footwear matters: Many paths are stone or gravel. Avoid flip-flops and wear sandals or sneakers with decent grip.

- Water and shade: Summers are hot—bring a refillable bottle. Public fountains are common in towns, less so in rural walks.

- Go slow: Part of the magic is unplanned. Don't rush your drive or your walk—stop at roadside cafés, dip into hidden coves, and talk to locals along the way.

Croatia and Montenegro aren't just places to see. They're places to move through—slowly, deliberately, with eyes open and camera maybe forgotten. Whether you're cruising cliffside roads or strolling hand-in-hand along the sea, these routes offer more than views—they offer perspective.

Chapter 5 – National Parks & Nature Trails

You could spend your whole trip along the Adriatic coast and have a fantastic time—but you'd be missing something essential if you skipped the inland landscapes. Croatia and Montenegro offer a rich range of national parks, nature preserves, and hiking trails that take you far from the crowds and into regions where nature is still wild, layered with history, and deeply tied to local identity.

This chapter focuses on the parks that make these countries stand out in Europe's ecological map—from Croatia's emerald lakes and canyon forests to Montenegro's rugged alpine ridges and wildlife-rich wetlands. Whether you're in it for a challenging climb or a peaceful walk past waterfalls and old shepherd huts, these protected areas offer more than scenery. They tell a story—of geology, tradition, resilience, and slow travel in its purest form.

5.1 Plitvice & Krka Waterfalls (Croatia)

A Tale of Water, Time, and Limestone

Nestled in central Croatia, Plitvice Lakes and Krka National Park showcase the country's geological heartbeat—water shaping limestone into magnificent cascades and tranquil emerald pools. But visiting them is about more than ticking off a "must-see" destination. It's stepping into landscapes where water has defined rhythm and heritage, carving out not just canyons and cascades, but stories woven through local culture for centuries.

While both parks celebrate waterfalls, each offers a distinct experience. Plitvice is a polished masterpiece: vast, serene, layered. Krka is looser, warmer, sociable—a place you can wade into and refresh yourself close to the cascades. One feels like wandering through a cathedral of nature; the other, an afternoon revel in its cool embrace.

Plitvice Lakes National Park: A Living Water Symphony

A Hydrological Masterpiece

Plitvice's magic comes from its sixteen lakes, cascading through limestone terraces in 90 stepping waterfalls. The park is carved into Upper and Lower zones, each revealing its own flavor. The Upper Lakes are quieter, shaded, forested; the Lower Lakes widen near towering cliffs, forming vistas that are dramatic and cinematic.

Wooden boardwalks wind through both areas, but planning your route is key. A full circuit—option H or K—takes 4–6 hours, offering a full sensory journey: gurgling brooks underfoot, shafts of light through trees, water splashing beside every step. I recommend starting early from Entrance 1 to catch the morning mist rising above turquoise waters—when stillness and soundscapes are raw.

Flora, Fauna & Karst

The karst environment means underwater volcanic caves, tufa barriers, and forest ecosystems rich in wildlife. Keep an eye out for deer in the woods—elusive but present—and butterflies that flicker around meadows in summer. With luck, you might even glimpse a rare bird: gems like the white-throated dipper live here.

Boardwalks invite slow observation. Pause by osier-fringed lakes, listen as water curls around moss and rock, and feel the impact of centuries of accumulation creating terraces and barriers. The water is so clear you'll see stones and leaves gleaming ten feet down.

History, Tourism & Conservation

Once a refuge during Ottoman raids, archaeological sites hint at early settlers. The lakes themselves are the latest chapter—forming gradually as moss and travertine built earthen dams. The park's modern story is one of survival: declared the country's first national park in 1949, resilience became literal in the 1990s war when bridges and facilities were damaged, then rebuilt with an eye toward both conservation and accessibility.

Visitors come in droves now, but boardwalk design carries traffic consciously, and strict no-swim rules in Plitvice help preserve what feels pristine—even as infrastructure supports tens of thousands annually.

Practical Tips

- Arrive before 8 a.m. to see sunrise over the lakes. Weekdays are quieter; avoid mid-June to August weekends.

- Wear grippy shoes and a light jacket (mornings are chilly, even in July).

- Eat packed lunches or buy food from entrance cafés—they're simple but hearty—so you can linger.

- If foot traffic is a concern, consider visiting out of season (April–May, September–October), weather permitting.

- Boats run between zones; learn the schedule and build a "floating pause" into your day.

- Photographers try midday light in the wooded Upper Lakes and golden light near Lower Lake cascades in late afternoon.

Krka National Park: Jump In Where History Meets River Life

Water You Can Touch

Krka is a river park. Instead of lakes joined by waterfalls, slow terraces break into larger drops. Skradinski Buk, the main reach, is wide, tiered, and gentle enough for swimming in designated spots—rare in protected areas. You can practically touch the cascades, paddle among floating lilies, and take a literal dip in the park.

Below the falls, restored mills recall centuries of traditional water-powered living. One now operates daily, grinding corn for fresh tortillas—or traditional *pogača*. Listening to the whir of wheel and waterfall confides a living craft.

Beyond the Big Falls

Boat trips take you upriver to Visovac Island, where a 15th-century Franciscan monastery sits under cypresses—an oasis of calm. Further upstream lie evocative smaller cascades: Roški Slap, with multi-tier steps and wider beaches, and Manojlovački Slapovi, even quieter. These feel like hidden chapters in Krka's story, away from crowds.

Bring a towel and swimwear if allowed in season (check updates): the water is cool, gentle, and precisely what justified a day of exploration.

Cultural Connection

Nearby Šibenik—a fortified coastal town—once served as the commerce node for fishermen who used Krka's waterways. You'll find visual echoes of maritime artistry in stone-fortified walls and cathedrals carved by Dalmatian stonemasons.

Practical Tips

- Best combination: morning at Plitvice, afternoon (or next day) at Krka, especially in summer.

- Follow signs carefully for swim zones—respect protected areas.

- Bringing a waterproof case or bag—river spray is part of the experience.

- Full-day tickets cover multiple entrances, making ferry rides both practical and scenic.

- Listen for Monk's chanting at Visovac—check with Franciscan guards for chapel access.

5.2 Paklenica & Lakeside Hikes

A Rocky Road Between Sea and Sky

While much of Croatia's interior is gentler, the Velebit Mountains, near Starigrad Paklenica on the coast, are rugged—vertical limestone walls that spill into the Adriatic. Paklenica National Park protects canyon floors, alpine ridges, and world-class cliffs. It's a land where Mediterranean herbs grow beneath ancient forest, where WW2 bunkers huddle under overhangs, and where mountaineers test their grit.

This is the kind of place you don't just visit—you earn.

Canyon Walks for Wanderers

Velika Paklenica: The Grand Entrance

The larger canyon, Velika Paklenica, begins with a wide, paved road flanked by pine. Walk half an hour, and the scenery tightens—the limestone monastery of rocks hovers overhead, sunlight flickering between cliffs. Creekside paths give way to gurgling pools and old mill ruins.

Past the burned-down mill at Mlinski Kuk, trails branch toward Planinarski Dom, a mountain hut perfect for a break. Hike a bit further and the canyon narrows more, opening toward high alpine terrain.

Mala Paklenica: Peace in Seclusion

Smaller, quieter, but just as dramatic, Mala Paklenica is rougher under foot. On quieter days, this gorge feels holy—the hush alone is worth the hike. Moss-covered walls drip water year-round. The absence of crowds gives the walk a personal rhythm—each step in silence, ripples of sound echoing.

Alpine Trails & Ridge Climbs

Youthful Peaks & Summits

Beyond the canyons lies a world of high mountain trails. Hiking up Bojin Kuk or heading toward Vaganski Vrh, the island's tallest peak (1,757 m), rewards with full-circle panoramas over the Adriatic and into Bosnia. This is no gentle climb—expect loose scree, established cairns, and a sense of elevation that invites both awe and altitude awareness.

Hiking Tips

- Day trips to huts such as Malovrisev dom or Dom u Velikoj Paklenici let you stretch overnight.

- Be warned: summer storms gather fast. Hike early, check weather, and carry waterproof shells and maps.

- Trail markings are visible but not always multilingual. A longer trek demands navigating using maps and landmarks, not signal coverage.

Lakeside Trails: Quiet Human-Nature Encounters

These quieter lakes aren't just substitutes—they offer a gentler way to connect while tapping local life.

Vransko Jezero

A freshwater lake near Zadar, encircled by wooded trails and birdwatching hides. Trails cross olive paths and connect to villages where farmers press oil and craft baskets. Early in the morning, local anglers test their patience on the banks. By noon, the sun flattens light, and trails feel steep with shine.

Trail suggestions:

- Short loop (3 km): From the Visitor Center to Kamenjak Viewpoint.

- Medium loop (7–10 km): South to old villages, up into pine shade.

- Birdwatcher's route: Follow signs to lookouts—binocular help if you have them.

Peruća Lake

Highland reservoir near Sinj with wooded trails and kayaking access. There are caves (explored via local guides), shaded shorelines and pulse-quiet waters. It's less traveled—bring water, and be prepared for basic trails.

Why Nature Trails Matter

1. **Local experience**
   Walk with villagers tending fig trees near Vransko. Float near fishermen's outboards at Paklenica's canyon entrance.

2. **Seasonal variety**
   Wildflowers carpet alpine ridges in spring. Fall brings golden haze in beech groves. Familiar places change character through the year.

3. **Ecological awareness**
   Learn about karst aquifers, endemic orchids like the *Orchis italica*, and rivers that connect inland springs to

saltwater seas.

4. **Self-paced challenges**
   Whether you're an occasional walker or a certified mountaineer, nature trails meet you where you are.

Practical Park Info

Park	Entrance	Best Months	Difficulty	Trail Gear	Notes
Plitvice	North & South	Apr–Jun, Sep–Oct	Easy–Moderate	Hiking shoes, layers	Boardwalks; no swimming
Krka	Lozovac	Apr–Jun, Sep–Oct	Easy	Swimwear (optional)	Swim zones near

						Skradinski Buk
Paklenica Velika	Entrance Paklenica	May–Oct	Moderate–Strenuous	Trekking boots & poles	Canyon hiking, watch for rain	
Vransko Jezero	Visitor Center	Apr–Sep	Easy	Comfortable wear	Bird hides; rural trails	
Peruća Lake	Near Sinj	Apr–Oct	Easy–Moderate	Trail shoes	Minimal services; local hospitality	

5.3 Durmitor & Tara Canyon (Montenegro)

Mountain Wilds and River Myths

Montenegro's north is a different world from its shimmering coastline. The shift is dramatic: from sea views and olives to alpine forests, glacial lakes, and sharp stone ridges. Durmitor National Park sits at the heart of this mountainous terrain, a UNESCO-protected expanse wrapped in legend and weathered beauty. Dominated by the limestone peaks of the Dinaric Alps, Durmitor is where hikers, climbers, and road-trippers find the raw pulse of Montenegro.

Threading through this region is the Tara River Canyon, Europe's deepest river gorge. If the coast shows Montenegro's elegance, the north shows its strength—a land of deep forests, ice-fed rivers, and people who've lived with the land rather than upon it.

Durmitor National Park: Rugged & Reflective

A National Treasure

The park covers over 390 square kilometers and includes 48 peaks above 2,000 meters. The tallest—Bobotov Kuk at 2,523 m—is climbable in summer by fit hikers. Even if you're not scaling summits, there are dozens of trails through meadows, pine forest, and along alpine ridgelines. It's a park that rewards curiosity and preparation, not casual tourism.

Spring through autumn is best for hiking. Snow lingers well into May, especially on northern slopes, and summer opens the full range of routes. Autumn brings golds and russets to the forested valleys—a quieter, cooler experience. Winters here are harsh but magical: the area transforms into a ski zone centered on Žabljak, the small town that serves as Durmitor's hub.

Crno Jezero (Black Lake)

This is Durmitor's most visited site, and it deserves the attention. Crno Jezero is a glacial lake ringed by forest and backed by towering peaks. In morning light, the water mirrors the mountains with uncanny clarity; in afternoon shade, it earns its name with near-black reflections. A walking path loops around the lake (just under 4 km), and from there, marked trails lead deeper into the park.

Stop at the lake café or bring a picnic—early mornings and evenings are peaceful, while midday in summer can get busy. The lake is fed by snowmelt and small springs; swimming isn't encouraged but often done informally near the edges in warmer months.

Beyond the Lake: Ridges, Meadows & Peaks

Some routes to consider:

- Škrka Valley Trail: Moderate to strenuous; passes alpine huts and leads to quieter glacial lakes. Highly scenic.

- Bobotov Kuk: Strenuous, requires a head for heights and sure footing. Reward: panoramic views from Montenegro's roof.

- Ice Cave (Ledena Pećina): Shorter but still demanding; bring a headlamp. Inside, frozen stalactites hang year-round.

The further you go from the lake, the fewer people you'll meet. Wildlife sightings are possible: chamois, golden eagles, even brown bears at extreme elevations—though rarely seen.

Tara Canyon: Europe's Deepest, Wildest Gorge

The River that Carved a Country

The Tara River has etched one of Europe's grandest canyons—1,300 meters deep in places, with cliffs wrapped in forests and mist. Designated a UNESCO Biosphere Reserve, the river is protected for its clean water and rare ecology.

If Durmitor is about hiking, Tara is about perspective: standing on the edge of something ancient and immense. The Đurđevića Tara Bridge, an engineering feat from the 1940s, offers an excellent panorama—especially striking in morning light. Walk across it, lean over the edge (if you can handle heights), and watch the river churn far below.

Whitewater Rafting & River Culture

Rafting on the Tara is a seasonal highlight—from late spring to early fall. The most popular stretch is from Brštanovica to

Šćepan Polje, with rapids rated Class II–IV depending on water levels. Outfitters in Žabljak and nearby towns arrange day or multi-day trips, often including overnight stays in rustic riverside lodges or camps.

Expect cold, clear water, narrow canyons, and quiet intervals between rapids where cliffs rise hundreds of meters on either side. It's both thrilling and humbling.

Rafting trips often include:

- Transport to the river and back
- All gear (wetsuit, helmet, etc.)
- Guides (typically fluent in English and well-trained)
- Meals featuring mountain dishes: stewed lamb, local cheese, fresh river fish

Even if you're not rafting, hiking trails and viewpoints line the upper canyon, especially near Dobrilovina Monastery and the old Roman bridge remains.

Žabljak: Base Camp with Mountain Charm

This small town isn't flashy, but it's welcoming and practical. Accommodation ranges from mountain chalets to hostels and family-run inns. Supermarkets are stocked, and there are good local eateries serving dishes like kačamak (cornmeal mash with cheese) or grilled river trout.

Public transport is limited, so renting a car gives you the freedom to explore lesser-known trailheads, especially if venturing south to Plužine or west to Piva Lake. Roads are winding but rewarding—with high plateaus, rock tunnels, and more sheep than traffic.

5.4 Lake Skadar & Biodiversity Trails

Wild Waters Between Mountains and Myth

Spilling across the Montenegro-Albania border, Lake Skadar is the Balkans' largest lake—and perhaps its most quietly compelling. It doesn't announce itself with towering peaks or dramatic cliffs. Instead, it wins visitors with a slow, unfolding richness: wetlands teeming with birds, ancient island monasteries, lily-covered shallows, and villages that still fish and farm in tune with the water.

Skadar is more than a lake—it's an ecosystem, a cultural patchwork, and a natural refuge. And it's one of Montenegro's best places to slow down and observe, rather than conquer.

The Landscape

The Montenegrin side of the lake is framed by the Rumija Mountains to the south and low-lying hills to the north, where wetlands stretch toward Podgorica. Virpazar is the main entry point—a small town with stone bridges, boat docks, and birdwatching stations. From there, you can book boat rides, rent kayaks, or hike the surrounding hills.

The lake's shape changes with the seasons. In summer, shallows dry and create reed islands; in spring, meltwater expands its surface dramatically, flooding meadows and revealing new wildlife habitats.

Birdwatching Paradise

Lake Skadar is home to over 280 bird species, including the rare Dalmatian pelican, glossy ibis, pygmy cormorant, and herons in abundance. It's one of the last strongholds for nesting pelicans in Europe and a top destination for ornithologists.

Spring and autumn migrations are peak times. Locals offer guided birding trips by boat—slowly gliding through reed beds, binoculars in hand, with silence as the soundtrack.

For casual visitors:

- Walk the Pančeva Oka loop: an easy 3–4 km wetland circuit.

- Visit the Miseluk observation tower, northeast of Virpazar.

- Explore early morning for best bird activity and golden light.

Historic Layers: Monasteries, Villages, and Ruins

Dotting the lake's islands are medieval Orthodox monasteries, most active but quiet, reached by boat. Beška Monastery, for example, offers views from a rocky island outcropping, with frescoes and quiet gardens. Kom Monastery, less visited, rewards those willing to hike or paddle.

In Rijeka Crnojevića, once the capital of Montenegro under Prince Danilo I, you'll find stone bridges, Ottoman ruins, and quiet riverfront walks. Renting a bike here and cycling the Cemetery Loop (a nickname, not a grim one) offers winding roads through vineyards and fig orchards.

Kayaking & Water Trails

Unlike rafting, kayaking Skadar is about ease and access. Routes vary in length and challenge:

- Virpazar to Lesendro Fortress: scenic, short, good for beginners
- Rijeka Crnojevića loop: longer, through clear tributaries with

    cliff-lined bends

- **Island monastery routes:** require local navigation help

Rental operators provide maps and drybags; bring sun protection and water.

Eco-Trails and Biodiversity Walks

Hiking around Skadar isn't about height—it's about discovery. Trails skirt vineyards, pass through forest, and connect to lookouts. One of the best:

- **Pavlova Strana Viewpoint Trail:** 5–6 km round trip from Rijeka Crnojevića; ends at a panorama above the lake's serpentine bends. Popular with photographers.

Others meander into villages like Godinje, where stone houses cluster into amphitheaters and locals press olive oil in centuries-old mills. Signs are basic, so bring an offline map or hike with a guide.

Food and Local Life

The lake shapes cuisine here: expect carp cooked in clay pots, eel stew, fresh cheeses from nearby farms, and wines produced along the southern slopes. The Vranac grape dominates—deep, earthy, and good value.

Family-owned restaurants like Konoba Badanj in Virpazar or Stari Most in Rijeka Crnojevića offer hearty meals after long walks or paddle days. Slow food isn't a movement here—it's tradition.

Travel Logistics

- Best base towns: Virpazar (for boat access), Rijeka Crnojevića (for quiet stays and biking), or Podgorica (for day trips).

- Best seasons: Late spring (birdwatching), early autumn (warm water, fewer insects).

- Getting around: Cars offer flexibility, but guided boat tours and bike rentals help reduce traffic and environmental strain.

- **Environmental etiquette:** Stick to marked trails, avoid loud noise near bird nesting zones, and support local eco-operators.

Chapter 6 – Adventure & Outdoor Thrills

Where Adrenaline Meets Landscape

Croatia and Montenegro are often praised for their coastlines, historic towns, and food—but for many travelers, the real highlight is movement. This region is packed with landscapes that invite action: rivers to paddle, cliffs to climb, trails to bike, and waters to sail. Adventure here is not an activity tacked onto a beach holiday—it's built into the geography. From highland ridges to deep canyons, from quiet bays to crashing rivers, the Balkans reward anyone ready to explore with their body, not just their camera.

This chapter focuses on outdoor activities that immerse you in the environment. It's for travelers who want to sweat a little, breathe in mountain air, or glide silently across a reed-filled lake. Whether you're a seasoned athlete or just curious to try something new, this section breaks down where to go, what to expect, and how to experience the best of Croatia and Montenegro's wild side.

6.1 Kayaking & Paddleboarding

A Different Kind of Horizon

For a region shaped so heavily by water, it's no surprise that some of its best adventures happen just above the surface. Kayaking and stand-up paddleboarding (SUP) offer a way to explore Croatia and Montenegro at eye level with the sea, the riverbanks, and the lake reeds. These aren't high-speed sports. They're about presence, rhythm, and seeing things you might miss from the road or shore.

Both countries offer a wide variety of paddling environments, from island-strewn archipelagos and sheltered bays to winding rivers and highland lakes. You don't need much experience—just a sense of balance and a willingness to get a little wet.

Sea Kayaking the Dalmatian Coast

One of the most accessible and beautiful ways to explore Croatia's coast is by kayak. The Dalmatian Islands, especially around Dubrovnik, Korčula, and Hvar, are ideal for half-day or multi-day trips.

From Dubrovnik, kayakers often launch from Pile Bay, hugging the ancient walls before crossing to Lokrum Island. The early morning light against the stone is unforgettable, and paddling into small caves beneath the cliffs gives a unique sense of scale.

Korčula offers a more laid-back route: circling the small islets off its southern shore, stopping to snorkel in hidden coves or picnic on empty beaches. Wind tends to pick up in the afternoon, so it's wise to start early.

If you're looking for a more structured experience, multi-day trips connect islands like Šipan, Mljet, and Pelješac, with overnight stays in small guesthouses or even beach camping with local guides.

Paddleboarding: Stillness and Sightlines

Stand-up paddleboarding has exploded in popularity across Croatia's calmer waters. It's especially good on:

- Lakes: Like Peruća Lake near Split or Vrana Lake on the Dalmatian coast.

- Sheltered bays: Near Cavtat, Ston, or the Pakleni Islands off Hvar.

- Morning coastlines: When the sea is glassy and winds are low.

SUP gives you a full-body workout, but it's also meditative. At sunrise, it's just you, the board, and the reflection of mountains or cliffs on the water. Boards can often be rented by the hour or day in beach towns—just ask around for calmer conditions and local tips.

Montenegro by Paddle

While Croatia's coastline gets more attention, Montenegro offers arguably more dramatic kayaking—especially in its lakes and rivers.

Lake Skadar is the go-to paddling destination, with routes from Virpazar looping through water lilies and pelican habitats. Bring binoculars or go with a guide to catch wildlife in the early morning hours.

On the Adriatic, Kotor Bay is a stunning place to kayak or paddleboard. The water is calm, the backdrop is mountainous, and there's no better way to approach towns like Perast or paddle to the islet of Our Lady of the Rocks.

For river kayaking, the Tara and Morača Rivers have stretches that suit intermediate paddlers. However, some areas are better suited to rafting due to stronger currents and rapids. Always check water levels and seasonal conditions.

Safety, Rentals & Skill Levels

You don't need to be an expert to enjoy paddling here, but conditions change fast—especially at sea. Wind and chop can come up by mid-afternoon. Stick to the shore unless you're with a guide or know the area well.

Rentals typically include:

- Life jackets (mandatory for rivers, strongly recommended at sea)

- Dry bags for valuables

- Basic instructions if you're new to the sport

If you're planning a longer trip, check the return policies—some places allow point-to-point journeys, others expect round trips.

For SUP, balance is key. Many first-timers start on their knees and work up to standing. Expect a learning curve—but also a lot of laughter.

Insider Tips

- Start early for calm waters and fewer boats.

- Use reef-safe sunscreen—especially in Lake Skadar, where the ecosystem is sensitive.

- Always carry water, a snack, and a hat. Even on overcast days, the glare can be intense.

- Talk to locals. Many fishermen and tour operators know the safest routes and can point you toward quiet spots.

6.2 Mountain Biking and Rock Climbing

Getting Off the Road—Literally

Croatia and Montenegro aren't just good for slow sightseeing—they're excellent for pushing your legs and lungs to the limit. Mountain biking here isn't just about the ride; it's about the landscape: rocky coastlines, steep switchbacks, rolling vineyards, and pine forests that open onto coastal views. Rock climbing, meanwhile, taps into the region's limestone cliffs, gorges, and hidden crags that have drawn climbers from across Europe.

The scene is growing fast. In both countries, local biking communities and climbing clubs are carving out trails, installing routes, and hosting meetups—often in towns that double as cultural destinations. You don't need to be extreme to get involved. You just need grit, curiosity, and a little planning.

Biking the Dalmatian Backroads

In Croatia, biking through the Dalmatian hinterland offers a completely different view of the country. Trails near Imotski, Makarska, and Sinj run through olive groves, vineyards, and karst terrain. These are rarely flat rides—but the scenery is often worth the effort.

For coastal mountain biking, Pelješac Peninsula is a favorite. Trails cut through pine forest, past quiet beaches, and offer ridgeline views toward the islands. Bring water—there are few services between towns.

Island biking is also a highlight. Brač offers both gravel trails and tough climbs, including the route up Vidova Gora, the highest island peak on the Adriatic. In Hvar, dirt roads connect lavender fields with tiny coves and sea views.

Most rentals are available in larger towns and island hubs. Look for proper gear—some shops offer full-suspension bikes and GPS trail apps.

Montenegro's Wild Rides

Montenegro's mountains make it a biker's playground. Near Durmitor, rugged trails surround Žabljak, leading through meadows and forest to panoramic viewpoints. You'll need a decent level of fitness—altitude and incline are part of the deal.

In the south, Lovćen National Park has highland trails with views down to the Bay of Kotor. One ride, from Ivanova Korita to Njeguši Village, is a favorite: pine-scented air, historic stone villages, and hairpin turns all the way down.

The Piva and Komovi regions are even more remote. If you're looking for bikepacking potential, this is where to go.

Climbing: From Deep Canyons to Craggy Coasts

Croatia's Paklenica National Park is the best-known climbing spot, with over 400 bolted routes on limestone faces above the

Velika Paklenica Gorge. Climbers of all levels find something here—from short sport climbs to long, multi-pitch adventures.

Montenegro's Tara Canyon has deep walls and bouldering areas around Dobrilovina and Đurđevića Tara. Stijena (near Podgorica) is growing in popularity with locals bolting new routes. The Bar area offers unique coastal climbing, where routes face the Adriatic and the sun sets on your belay.

Gear can be rented in national park hubs, but experienced climbers often bring their own. Guide services are available for newcomers, and routes are increasingly well-marked and maintained.

Practical Notes

- Skill Level: Most bike trails and climbing areas range from intermediate to expert. Beginners should start with a guide or group.

- Best Seasons: Spring and autumn are ideal. Summer can be too hot, especially inland. Winter brings snow to higher altitudes—great for fat biking, but tough for traditional rides.

- Safety: Cell signal is limited in remote areas. Always let someone know your route. Use proper helmets and check gear conditions.

6.3 Zip-lining, Rafting, and Cave Tours

Adventure that Moves You—Fast and Deep

Not every adventure in Croatia and Montenegro requires days of hiking or hours of paddling. Some happen in sharp, adrenaline-filled bursts—in the air, on rushing rivers, or underground in ancient limestone. This part of the Balkans is laced with gorges, rivers, and karst terrain, making it one of the most geographically exciting regions for short but high-impact outdoor experiences.

Zip-lining, whitewater rafting, and caving all draw on the region's natural infrastructure.

These aren't manufactured thrill parks; they're rooted in real geography—places where people once moved timber or hunted, now reimagined for adventure tourism. You'll find yourself skimming above canyons, crashing through rapids, or inching through narrow caves lit only by your headlamp.

Zip-lining: Speed Meets Scenery

Zip-lining has grown rapidly across Croatia and Montenegro, thanks to the abundance of deep canyons and rugged mountains. But don't expect jungle-style courses or amusement park setups—here, the focus is often a single, epic line with a view you won't forget.

One of the longest and most popular zip-lines in the region is the Tara Canyon Zipline near the Đurđevića Tara Bridge in Montenegro. You'll be strapped in and sent flying over one of Europe's deepest canyons, with the turquoise Tara River raging hundreds of meters below. It's fast (up to 50–70 km/h), it's scenic, and it's surprisingly accessible—you can drive right up to the launch point.

In Croatia, the CetinA River zip-line near Omiš is another highlight. The full course involves multiple lines, including one that stretches over 700 meters across a dramatic river gorge. It's a thrilling complement to any coastal trip—especially if you're staying near Split.

Most zip-line operators provide all gear and short safety briefings. Weight and age limits apply, but many first-timers describe it as more exhilarating than scary.

Rafting the Region's Wild Rivers

If zip-lining is about air, rafting is about water—and the rivers here deliver. Montenegro, in particular, has some of the best whitewater in Europe.

The Tara River, within Durmitor National Park, is the most famous rafting destination in the Balkans. Flowing through steep limestone cliffs and dense forest, it's known for both its Class III-IV rapids and its startling clarity (locals call it the "tear of Europe"). Most rafting trips cover a 10–20 km stretch of the river, with breaks to swim in icy pools or jump from river boulders. Spring and early summer (May to early

July) are peak rafting months, when snowmelt swells the river.

Croatia offers gentler rafting experiences, especially around the Cetina River near Omiš, which is ideal for beginners or families. The river cuts through cliffs and tunnels beneath hanging vegetation, with a few light rapids to keep things fun. Some tours even combine rafting with canyoning—rappelling down waterfalls and sliding into narrow pools.

Guides are mandatory on most rivers, both for safety and navigation. They also offer local stories and tips, which can add a human layer to the natural drama.

Going Underground: Caves and Caverns

This part of the Balkans is riddled with caves—some used by Neolithic humans, others by bats, monks, or resistance fighters. Today, many are accessible with guides, giving travelers a rare chance to descend into the region's geological history.

One standout is Vjetrenica Cave in southern Bosnia and Herzegovina (an easy day trip from Dubrovnik). This is the largest cave system in the Dinaric Alps, with illuminated tunnels and sightings of the olm, a blind aquatic salamander endemic to the area.

In Montenegro, the Lipa Cave near Cetinje is the most accessible and visitor-friendly. Guided tours lead you deep into karst chambers, past stalagmites, pools, and ancient limestone formations. It's a cool, eerie contrast to the summer heat—bring a jacket, even in July.

While some caves can be explored on foot, others require helmets, lamps, and climbing or crawling. Serious spelunkers may want to look into multi-hour or overnight expeditions, especially in less-touristed parts of Montenegro's north.

What to Know

- Weather matters. Zip-lining and rafting are weather-sensitive. Always confirm trips the day before, especially in shoulder seasons.

- Bring basics. A dry change of clothes for rafting, closed-toe shoes for caves, and layers for cold air are essential.

- Guides make the difference. Not just for safety—but for storytelling. Many are locals who know the landscape's history inside and out.

Whether you're flying over a canyon, diving into rapids, or ducking into the belly of the earth, this section of the Balkans will move you—in every sense.

6.4 Coastal Sailing and Diving

The Adriatic From Below and Above

It's impossible to talk about outdoor adventure in Croatia and Montenegro without talking about the sea. The Adriatic isn't just a pretty backdrop; it's a playground, a historical route, and a key part of life on the coast. For travelers who want more than a beach chair, sailing and diving are two of the most rewarding ways to engage with this landscape.

Sailing lets you explore archipelagos, swim in inaccessible coves, and watch sunset from the deck with nothing but the sound of waves. Diving, meanwhile, reveals what's beneath the surface: reefs, wrecks, underwater caves, and marine life that changes from bay to bay. Both are immersive. Both can shift your relationship with the Adriatic.

Sailing Croatia's Island Chains

Croatia's coastline is famously jagged, with over 1,200 islands and islets. For sailors, it's a paradise of short hops, reliable winds, and well-serviced marinas. But even if you don't have a license or experience, it's easy to get on the water—charter trips range from luxury catamarans to local skippers with traditional wooden boats.

Popular sailing routes include:

- Split to Dubrovnik: Island-hopping through Hvar, Vis, Korčula, and the Elaphiti Islands.

- Zadar to Šibenik: Navigating the Kornati Archipelago, a national park of barren, windswept islands and secret bays.

- **Rovinj to Pula (Istria):** Less crowded, with Roman ruins, sleepy ports, and excellent food stops.

Some routes focus on nature, others on nightlife, but the beauty is in the flexibility. You can tailor a trip for quiet beaches, historic towns, or remote anchorages where stars outnumber people.

Shorter options—sunset cruises, half-day island trips, or skippered day sails—are also widely available, especially from Split, Hvar Town, Dubrovnik, and Trogir.

Montenegro by Boat

Montenegro has fewer islands but makes up for it with fjord-like bays and dramatic coastline. Kotor Bay is the jewel: a sheltered, mountain-ringed expanse where even a short boat ride feels cinematic. Renting a small motorboat or joining a sailboat tour gives access to places like:

- Perast and Our Lady of the Rocks

- Submarine caves near Rose

- Secluded beaches between Herceg Novi and Budva

Farther south, sailing the coast from Bar to Ulcinj gives you views of old forts, long beaches, and stretches of undeveloped shore.

While Montenegro's sailing scene is smaller than Croatia's, it's growing—and often less crowded. The Porto Montenegro marina in Tivat also serves as a hub for charter trips and boat rentals.

Diving the Adriatic: Reefs, Wrecks, and Walls

The Adriatic isn't a coral-rich sea like the tropics, but it has clear waters, strong biodiversity, and plenty of dive-worthy history beneath the surface. Especially around wrecks and reefs, marine life tends to concentrate: octopus, sea bream, conger eels, and nudibranchs are all common.

Top dive locations in Croatia include:

- **Vis Island:** Known for WWII shipwrecks and excellent visibility. The wreck of the B-17 Flying Fortress is a highlight for advanced divers.

- **Kornati National Park:** Vertical walls, caves, and drop-offs rich in fish.

- **Mljet:** Calm, clear waters with underwater springs and rock formations.

Dive shops operate in most major coastal towns and on the larger islands. Certification is required for deeper dives, but many operators offer beginner sessions in shallow bays.

In Montenegro, the coastline between Budva and Petrovac has promising dive sites, including the wreck of the Austrian steamer Tihany, plus several underwater caves. The dive scene is smaller, but the potential is huge—especially for travelers who value low-key, less-touristed experiences.

Essentials for Sea-Based Adventures

- **Licensing:** You'll need certification to rent a boat or dive unsupervised. Day sails and guided dives don't require prior experience.

- Packing tips: Quick-dry clothing, a waterproof bag, reef-safe sunscreen, and motion sickness bands (if prone) go a long way.

- Seasons: Late May through early October is prime sailing and diving season. Water is warmest in August and September.

From above the surface or below it, the Adriatic invites you to move—to steer, to explore, to submerge. It's not just a body of water; it's a living, shifting adventure.

Chapter 7 – Culture & Authentic Experiences

For many travelers, the real magic of Croatia and Montenegro isn't just in the views—though those are plenty impressive—it's in the moments of cultural connection: hearing a klapa group sing in a stone alleyway, stumbling into a tiny village festival, or sitting down to a meal cooked the same way it's been done for generations. This chapter is all about those kinds of experiences—where history, community, and creativity come to life.

Here, you'll find a wide-angle look at the region's festivals, artistic traditions, and layered history. Whether you're chasing the beat of summer music festivals, curious about ancient architecture, or interested in connecting with locals through food and storytelling, this section will help you understand what gives these coastal countries their deep, distinct sense of identity—and how you can experience it for yourself, respectfully and meaningfully.

7.1 Festivals, Music, and Local Traditions

The Rhythm of the Region

Croatia and Montenegro may be known for their dramatic coastlines, but they're just as rich in rhythm and ritual. Cultural festivals aren't just tourist events—they're part of the social fabric. Many are rooted in seasonal changes, saint days, or harvest cycles, while others celebrate music, theater, or regional identity. For travelers, they offer a front-row seat to local life—and often a chance to participate.

In both countries, festivals can pop up in major cities or tiny villages, often with little formal publicity. You might be walking through a square in late July and find a brass band setting up, or wander into a village and get handed a plate of grilled lamb or a glass of homemade rakija. These moments are spontaneous, communal, and often surprisingly intimate.

Music: From Klapa to Kolo

Croatia's musical traditions are deeply tied to place. On the Dalmatian coast, the most iconic form is klapa—a style of a cappella singing usually performed by male vocal groups. The songs are often melancholic, centered around love, the sea, and longing. Klapa performances are especially common in coastal towns like Split, Šibenik, and Trogir, particularly in the summer months. You might catch a group rehearsing in a stone alley, using the acoustics of the old walls as their amplifier.

Inland, you're more likely to encounter tamburica music—stringed instruments played in ensembles, especially during folk festivals in Slavonia. Montenegro, on the other hand, has a more rugged musical heritage, with strong influences from both the Balkans and the Ottoman past. The gusle, a single-stringed instrument, accompanies epic storytelling—poetic recitations of battles, ancestors, or folklore.

Dance is another key tradition. The kolo (circle dance) appears in both countries, usually during community gatherings or weddings. It's not performative in a theatrical sense—it's about inclusion, rhythm, and community.

Major Cultural Festivals

Throughout the year, cities and towns across the region host festivals that range from massive productions to hyperlocal celebrations. Some notable ones include:

- Dubrovnik Summer Festival (Croatia): Held each July and August, this event brings classical music, theater, and dance to the city's old streets, fortresses, and squares. The open-air venues—lit by torches or under the stars—make it especially memorable.

- KotorArt (Montenegro): A multidisciplinary festival that includes classical music, local art, and theater, all set against the backdrop of Kotor's medieval architecture.

- Sinjska Alka (Croatia): Held annually in the town of Sinj, this is a reenactment of a historic knightly tournament. Riders in full traditional dress gallop on horseback, aiming lances at a metal ring—honoring a 1715 victory over the Ottomans.

- Mimoza Festival (Montenegro): Taking place in Herceg Novi in

February, this festival celebrates the early bloom of mimosa flowers, with parades, music, seafood feasts, and cultural performances.

Many smaller towns also hold patron saint days, grape harvest celebrations, or coastal regattas that turn into all-day festivals. Tourists are often welcome—just follow the sound of live music or the smell of roasting meat.

Living Traditions

Not all traditions are tied to festivals. Some are woven into daily life. Watch how locals pour coffee slowly, chat with strangers on benches, or take evening walks through their neighborhood (the špica or promenade). In smaller towns, traditional dress still appears at weddings, christenings, or major community events. Food rituals—like slow-cooked peka, homemade rakija, or dried fig preserves—are cultural expressions as much as culinary ones.

Wherever you go, be curious but respectful. If you're invited to join a toast or a dance, say yes—it's the kind of cultural experience that can't be booked or bought, and it's almost always offered in the spirit of genuine hospitality.

7.2 Historical Depth: Roman, Venetian, Ottoman Legacies

A Region Shaped by Empires

To walk through Croatia or Montenegro is to move through layers of history. Cities here weren't just built—they were rebuilt, reimagined, and reclaimed by different empires, each leaving behind stones, styles, and stories. Roman emperors, Venetian merchants, Ottoman governors—all left their imprint. And unlike in many parts of Europe, these layers weren't entirely erased or rebuilt over. They coexist, side by side, in churches, mosques, palaces, and plazas.

Understanding this history adds incredible depth to your visit. That ornate doorway or sunken column? It might date back 1,000 years. The spiral street layout of an old town? That's likely Venetian. The presence of a mosque, just down the street from a Catholic church and an Orthodox cathedral?

That's the Balkan story—diverse, layered, and often contested.

Roman Roots

Croatia is dotted with Roman ruins, some grand, others tucked into modern neighborhoods. The best known is Diocletian's Palace in Split—built in the 4th century by Emperor Diocletian as his retirement residence. Unlike most ancient sites, this one isn't frozen in time—it's alive. People live, shop, and eat inside the palace walls, which makes the site feel less like a museum and more like a living relic.

Other Roman highlights include the Pula Arena, one of the most complete Roman amphitheaters in existence, and Salona, near Split, once a thriving Roman city now in ruins but still evocative in its layout and tombs.

Venetian Influence

The Venetian Republic controlled large parts of the Adriatic coast from the 15th to 18th centuries, especially Dalmatia. This influence is especially visible in places like

Zadar, Šibenik, Hvar, and Korčula, where loggias, bell towers, and stone alleys reflect Italian Gothic and Renaissance styles. In Kotor and Perast, you'll find similar Venetian façades—many built by wealthy merchant families under Venetian rule.

What's interesting is how these coastal cities adapted Venetian architecture to local needs: narrower streets for shade, water collection systems for dry summers, and fortress designs to ward off Ottoman invasions.

The Ottoman Legacy

Inland and in the south, the Ottoman Empire left a very different imprint. Bosnia and Herzegovina was part of the Ottoman realm for centuries, and its culture bled into southern Croatia and Montenegro, especially around Skadar Lake and Pljevlja. You'll see slender minarets, hammams, and Ottoman bridges that remain functional today.

Stari Bar in Montenegro is one of the most atmospheric places to explore Ottoman ruins—an abandoned hillside city with mosque arches, stone homes, and wild fig trees growing from the cracks.

Even local cuisine reflects Ottoman influence: burek (filled pastry), dolma (stuffed vegetables), and strong, unfiltered Turkish-style coffee are all part of daily life, particularly inland.

A Living History

While it's easy to think of this history as ancient, it's still active in identity and politics today. Talk to locals and you'll find pride in regional history—not just national identity. A Croatian from Istria might talk about their Austro-Hungarian roots, while someone from Kotor will mention their Venetian ancestors. These layers matter. They shape language, food, architecture, and even humor.

As a traveler, being aware of this complexity—rather than flattening it into a single "Balkan" story—helps you understand the pride, tension, and richness that shape the cultural landscape. Take time to read plaques, ask questions, and linger in the small museums and side streets. They often hold the deepest stories.

7.3 Art, Galleries & Film Events

Creativity Rooted in Place

Art in Croatia and Montenegro isn't confined to galleries. It spills into streets, cliffsides, festivals, and abandoned fortresses. From centuries-old religious frescoes to contemporary street murals, the region's artistic identity is constantly evolving—and often deeply political, personal, and tied to place.

Travelers who look beyond the "sun and sea" brochures will find a surprisingly vibrant cultural scene. Cities like Zagreb, Rijeka, Dubrovnik, Kotor, and Cetinje have established institutions, but even small towns can surprise you with pop-up exhibitions, community art spaces, or artist cooperatives.

What stands out most is the connection between the art and the landscape—paintings that capture the harsh beauty of the Dinaric Alps, sculptures that seem to rise out of limestone ruins, photography that reflects the shadows of war and rebuilding. For visitors interested in local narratives, contemporary art here offers something far more intimate than postcard views.

Galleries and Museums Worth Exploring

Zagreb, Croatia's capital, is the cultural powerhouse of the country. You'll find everything from the Museum of Contemporary Art (MSU)—a massive, modern space in Novi Zagreb—to quirky spots like the Museum of Broken Relationships, which uses donated objects and personal stories to explore human connections. Galleries like Galerija Klovićevi Dvori or Lauba showcase everything from classical painting to avant-garde installation.

Dubrovnik, better known for its medieval stone streets and seaside drama, also hosts excellent exhibitions. The Museum of Modern Art Dubrovnik (MOMAD) sits in a historic villa with sweeping sea views and a collection that focuses on 20th-century Croatian painters and sculptors. The contrast between setting and subject—baroque arches and abstract canvases—feels intentional.

In Montenegro, head to Cetinje, the country's old royal capital, to explore the National Museum complex, which houses historical archives alongside impressive collections of Montenegrin and Yugoslav art. Podgorica, often bypassed by tourists, has a growing arts scene driven by younger creatives and independent collectives. Small galleries like Galerija Art and occasional open-studio events give visitors a chance to see how modern artists are interpreting post-socialist identity.

Public Art and Street Murals

Especially in Croatia's inland or post-industrial towns like Rijeka, street art is both political and deeply expressive. In some areas, it's commentary on war, nationalism, or environmental loss. In others, it's playful and experimental. Split has developed a distinct urban art scene around its student population, with murals tucked between Roman ruins and crumbling socialist housing blocks.

Montenegro's seaside towns are more subtle, but in places like Ulcinj or Bar, you'll sometimes find Arabic calligraphy or poetic graffiti on walls near Ottoman-era ruins—layered expressions of the region's multi-ethnic past.

Film as a Cultural Bridge

Film plays a major role in how these countries process history, identity, and trauma. Local cinema often avoids commercial gloss, focusing instead on character-driven, sometimes dark or surreal stories. If you're in town during a film festival, go—it's a powerful window into the region's emotional core.

- Pula Film Festival (Croatia): Held inside a Roman amphitheater, this is one of the oldest film festivals in Europe. It screens a mix of Croatian and international films, with a strong emphasis on regional directors and stories.

- Motovun Film Festival: This hilltop town in Istria transforms each summer into a multi-day film party. The atmosphere is informal, the films are often provocative or experimental, and the setting—cobbled alleys and starry skies—makes it all feel cinematic.

- Kotor Art Cinema (Montenegro): A smaller but influential festival focused on indie cinema and documentaries. Screenings often take place in open-air courtyards or historical buildings, adding to the experience.

- UnderhillFest (Podgorica): Dedicated to documentaries, this festival highlights stories that challenge assumptions—about the Balkans and beyond.

If you miss a festival, you can still catch local films in art cinemas like Kinoteka Zagreb or Cadmus Cineplex in Budva. These venues occasionally offer English-subtitled screenings and are good spots to get a sense of local taste and storytelling.

Supporting Local Creatives

Many artists in both countries work independently or through informal networks. Look for local art fairs, student exhibitions, or handmade design shops. In places like Zagreb's Martićeva Street, Dubrovnik's War Photo Limited, or Kotor's small galleries, you can buy directly from the creators—whether that's a painting, a photo print, or a hand-bound journal.

These purchases don't just make for more meaningful souvenirs—they help sustain the region's vibrant but often underfunded creative ecosystem.

7.4 Learning from Locals, Community Tourism

Rethinking Travel Through Human Connection

One of the most memorable parts of traveling in Croatia and Montenegro is the conversations you'll have—often spontaneous, sometimes over a shared drink or during a long walk through a village orchard. Locals across both countries are often proud of their region, curious about visitors, and eager to share what they love about their home. But beyond casual interactions, a growing number of opportunities exist to learn more intentionally from the people who live and work in these places.

Community-based tourism is slowly gaining traction here—not in big organized tours, but through home-hosted meals, rural workshops, family-run guesthouses, and co-ops trying to keep traditional practices alive. For travelers interested in deeper cultural exchange, these experiences offer something that can't be replicated in a hotel lobby or gift shop.

Farmstays and Traditional Workshops

In rural Croatia, particularly in Slavonia, Lika, and Istria, families have opened their farms and kitchens to guests. These aren't polished resort experiences. You might be helping harvest plums, learning how to pickle vegetables, or baking pogača (traditional bread) in a wood-fired oven. Accommodations range from simple rooms to rustic cottages, and the meals are often seasonal, hyper-local, and hearty.

Montenegro has similar setups in areas like Durmitor, Bjelasica, and around Lake Skadar. Many villages here are slowly reviving traditional crafts—wool weaving, rakija distilling, herbal medicine—often with support from NGOs or diaspora initiatives. By joining a workshop, visitors directly support these efforts and get to hear the stories behind the skills.

Language, Humor, and Perspective

While English is widely spoken in tourist hubs, smaller towns and rural areas often rely on gestures, good humor, and patience. Learning a few words in Croatian or Montenegrin—"hvala" (thank you), "dobar dan" (good day), "molim" (please/you're welcome)—goes a long way. Locals often appreciate the effort and may even teach you a few slang terms or regional sayings.

Conversation also reveals cultural nuance. Humor here is often dry, sarcastic, and self-deprecating. There's a strong sense of identity but also a wariness of politics and bureaucracy. Don't be surprised if a friendly chat veers into history, food, and a critique of the EU, all in one sitting.

Homestays and Heritage Projects

Programs like etno villages—clusters of traditional homes restored for tourism—are gaining popularity. Some are more commercialized, but others are genuine efforts to preserve vanishing architectural styles and ways of life. Look for villages in Konavle, Herzegovina, or northern Montenegro, where stone cottages, watermills, and smokehouses are still part of daily life.

In places like Šibenik, Vis, or Kolašin, you'll also find community-run heritage museums or oral history projects—usually in small rooms, run by volunteers. These aren't polished institutions, but they often hold rare photographs, family objects, and local stories that give depth to your understanding of the place.

Travel With Respect

Finally, learning from locals means recognizing that you're a guest—not just in someone's home or workshop, but in their broader culture. Ask before taking photos, be generous with your attention and your time, and don't reduce complex histories to stereotypes. If someone invites you to dinner, it's not just a transaction—it's a sign of trust. Respect it. Share your own story, too. These exchanges, built on mutual curiosity, are often what travelers remember most.

Chapter 8 – Food, Wine & Local Flavors

Food in Croatia and Montenegro is more than just a meal—it's a reflection of geography, history, and local pride. From island taverns to hillside wineries, this region rewards those who travel with their tastebuds. Whether you're sitting down to a seafood platter overlooking the Adriatic or sampling homemade cheese in a mountain village, the flavors are tied to land and season. Ingredients are often humble, but technique and tradition elevate even the simplest dishes. In both countries, meals are social, unrushed, and rich with meaning.

This chapter takes you through the culinary highlights of the region, focusing not only on what to eat and drink but where and why. You'll learn how Croatian olive oil competes with the best in the world, why Montenegrin wines are finally gaining international attention, and where to find authentic rakija without a label. We'll also touch on local markets, modern food trends, and routes for travelers who want to follow the trail from vineyard to table—or truffle to toast.

8.1 Croatian Seafood, Truffles & Olive Oil Trails

The Adriatic on a Plate

Croatia's 1,000-plus islands and long Adriatic coastline shape its seafood traditions. Here, the cooking is restrained in the best way—designed to showcase what's fresh, not smother it. Expect grilled fish (usually whole, with skin and bones), mussels in white wine and garlic, octopus salad, and cuttlefish ink risotto. Simplicity is the rule, especially along the Dalmatian Coast.

The freshest catches often don't make it onto formal menus. Instead, they appear on handwritten chalkboards or are offered by waiters who say, "Today we have dentex, sea bass, maybe a little scorpionfish." If you're near a working harbor like Komiža, Ston, or Vela Luka, early mornings are a chance to see boats unloading their hauls—then eat that same fish by lunch.

In inland areas, freshwater dishes like trout and frog legs appear more often, but on the coast, seafood is the centerpiece. Look for buzara-style mussels or scampi, cooked in a light broth of wine, garlic, and herbs. Avoid tourist-trap menus promising "seafood mix" and instead ask what's local or seasonal. In many taverns (konobe), you can choose your fish by weight, and they'll grill it whole over wood coals.

Istria: Truffle Country

Northwest Croatia's Istrian Peninsula is one of Europe's truffle capitals. While Italy often dominates the spotlight, Istrian truffles—especially the white variety found near Motovun—are just as aromatic and sometimes even more potent. Truffle season runs from September to December for white truffles, and almost year-round for black ones.

Many family-run estates offer truffle hunting excursions, typically with a trained dog and followed by a rustic lunch featuring the morning's find. Even if you skip the muddy boots, you can sample truffles shaved over pasta, eggs, or even ice cream in towns like Buzet and Livade. Locally made truffle oils, spreads, and cheeses are widely available and make excellent edible souvenirs—but check the labels; not all are made with real truffles.

Olive Oil: Liquid Gold

Croatia's olive oil—especially from Istria and Dalmatia—has quietly been winning international awards, often beating out better-known Mediterranean producers. The secret? Small-scale operations, indigenous olive varieties, and traditional hand-harvesting methods. Tasting Croatian oil is a sensory experience: grassy, peppery, sometimes slightly bitter, with a finish that warms the throat.

Visitors can tour many uljare (olive mills), particularly in Istria where agrotourism is well developed. Places like Chiavalon, Ipsa, and Zigante offer guided tastings, harvest experiences, and insights into olive varieties. These visits also help support a sector that's vulnerable to climate change and economic shifts, especially for younger producers trying to keep family groves alive.

Don't expect olive oil to be free in restaurants—it's considered premium and often comes at a price. But if you're served house-made oil with bread, treat it with the same respect you'd give wine. Dip, swirl, taste slowly.

Where to Savor it All

For full immersion, follow one of Croatia's culinary roads, often marked with signs that read "wine & olive oil route" or put vina i ulja. In Istria and Pelješac, these trails wind through hilltop villages, vineyards, and estates. They're ideal for travelers who want to drive at a slow pace, meet producers face-to-face, and understand how geography influences taste.

In Dalmatia, food festivals and village feasts (feste) celebrate the seasonal calendar—anchovy season in May, squid festivals in autumn, olive harvest in November. These aren't tourist spectacles; they're community gatherings, often with music, dancing, and bottomless plates.

If you're traveling by ferry or island-hopping, ask about konobe run by fishing families—some serve only a handful of guests per night and cook what they caught that morning. It's these small, personal meals, eaten without a menu and served with a homemade glass of wine, that leave the most lasting memories.

8.2 Montenegrin Rakija, Wines & Cheeses

Rakija: More Than a Drink

In Montenegro, rakija is more than a national spirit—it's a symbol of hospitality, heritage, and social glue. Made from distilled fruit (typically grapes, plums, or figs), rakija is poured at nearly every occasion: weddings, funerals, casual visits, even business meetings. It's rarely bought in stores. Instead, it's made in backyard stills, passed down through families, and served in recycled bottles with no label.

Tasting rakija isn't about volume; it's about context. You'll often be offered a shot with a smile and a toast—živjeli or uzdravlje. Accept it if you can, but sip slowly. The proof is often higher than commercial spirits, and locals pride themselves on the purity and potency of their homemade versions.

In rural Montenegro, especially in Crmnica, Plužine, or Bijelo Polje, you'll sometimes see roadside signs offering domaći rakija (homemade rakija). Don't judge the operation by its size—some of the best comes from tiny stills next to chicken coops or grape trellises.

Wines: Hidden Strengths

Montenegro has one of the largest vineyards in Europe—Plantaže, near Podgorica—yet it remains relatively unknown on the global wine stage. The signature red grape is Vranac, a bold, deeply colored varietal with notes of dark berries and spice. White wines like Krstač and Žižak are rarer but worth seeking out, especially with seafood or cheese.

Wine tourism in Montenegro is expanding, with boutique estates like Bogojevic, Radevic, and Vukmirovic offering tastings in stunning countryside settings. Many are family-run, and the experience includes cellar tours, homemade snacks, and casual conversation about weather, harvests, and village gossip.

If you visit during harvest (typically September), some wineries allow guests to participate in grape picking or crushing. It's a great way to understand the rhythm of agricultural life—and you'll probably leave with a bottle or two under your arm, still warm from the sun.

Cheeses That Tell a Story

Montenegrin cheese is a quiet hero of the national kitchen. From Njeguški sir, a semi-hard smoked cheese from the mountains near Kotor, to fresh cow and goat cheeses from Plav, each variety reflects its terrain. These aren't factory-made blocks; they're living products, often shaped by microclimate, diet, and centuries of local practice.

At traditional markets or roadside stands, look for cheeses stored in olive oil jars or wrapped in cloth. Many are aged in caves or wooden boxes, resulting in flavors that range from creamy and mild to funky and sharp. Pair them with local honey or cured meats, and you've got a perfect picnic.

Some villages—especially in the Durmitor or Bjelasica regions—offer cheese-making workshops or tasting walks through mountain pastures. These experiences give travelers a better understanding of food traditions that are still at risk from depopulation and modern pressures.

Hospitality Over Hype

Montenegrin food and drink culture isn't about polished presentation or gourmet labels. It's about sitting down, staying a while, and letting the host guide the meal. Whether you're sharing shots of rakija with a beekeeper or sampling cheese in a shepherd's hut, the common thread is authenticity—unforced, rooted, and unforgettable.

8.3 Markets, Street Food & Vegan Options

The Pulse of the Market

If you want to get a feel for how people in Croatia and Montenegro live, eat, and talk, go to the local market—early, and with an open mind. Every town, no matter how small, usually has a green market (pijaca in Montenegro, tržnica in Croatia) that functions as both a shopping hub and a social hangout. These are not just for produce; they're cultural spaces where conversations flow over tables piled with seasonal fruit, homemade rakija in repurposed soda bottles, and sacks of dried herbs collected by hand.

Markets in larger towns like Zagreb's Dolac, Split's Pazar, Dubrovnik's Gundulićeva, or Kotor's Old Town market are bigger and busier, but the rules are the same. Arrive early to catch the best produce and watch the rhythm of local life. Vendors are often talkative, offering tastings, recommendations, or snippets of family history. If you show genuine interest, someone will probably slip you a sprig of fresh rosemary or a free fig "for the road."

Markets also reflect the calendar. In May, tables overflow with wild asparagus and cherries; in September, there are crates of grapes and foraged mushrooms. In winter, you'll find pickled cabbage, cured meats, and robust cheeses—food that was made to last through mountain winters and quiet coastal off-seasons.

Street Food, the Balkan Way

Croatia and Montenegro don't have a strong tradition of street food in the way of, say, Southeast Asia or Mexico. That said, snack culture is alive and well—especially around bakeries (pekare), grill shacks, ferry docks, and late-night kiosks. For quick bites that locals swear by, keep your eyes open and your expectations unpretentious.

In Croatia, you'll often see people lined up outside bakeries in the morning, grabbing a burek—a flaky phyllo pastry filled with cheese, meat, spinach, or even potato. It's filling, cheap, and travels well, making it perfect for bus rides or ferry days. Some of the best burek is found not in fancy cafés but in tiny bakeries with no name and no seating.

In Montenegro, grilled meat plays a big role in the snack scene. Look for ćevapi (small skinless sausages) or pljeskavica (a flat, spicy meat patty, often served in a warm flatbread with onions, kajmak cheese, and a dash of ajvar). While not technically street food, these can be found at fast-casual joints and roadside stalls called roštiljarnice, and they're deeply satisfying after a day of hiking or swimming.

Pizza slices, fried sardines, and seafood skewers also pop up near tourist beaches, especially in Dalmatia. While quality varies, if there's a long line of locals and the oil smells fresh, it's probably worth a try.

Vegetarian and Vegan in the Balkans

Historically, the region's cuisine has been very meat- and dairy-heavy—linked to its rural, mountainous lifestyle and strong pastoral traditions. That said, things are changing. In bigger cities like Zagreb, Split, Dubrovnik, Kotor, and Podgorica, you'll find dedicated vegetarian and vegan restaurants, as well as plenty of modern cafés that cater to plant-based diets with creativity and care.

Even outside major towns, there are often good options if you know what to ask for. Traditional dishes like blitva s krumpirom (Swiss chard with potatoes and olive oil), grah (bean stew), punjene paprike (stuffed peppers, often with rice and no meat), and various salate (salads) can be found on most menus. Dalmatian grilled vegetables, marinated olives, and fresh bread with local olive oil are also easy to come by.

Be cautious with soups or stews—they often start with a meat-based broth, even if no meat is visible. It's best to ask: *"Je li ovo bez mesa?"* (Is this without meat?) or *"Imate li nešto vegansko?"* (Do you have anything vegan?). In Montenegro, people may interpret "vegetarian" to mean "no pork," so be clear about your needs.

In smaller towns and villages, the selection may be limited, but hosts are often accommodating if given notice. If you're staying in a sobe (guesthouse) or agriturismo-style lodging, consider reaching out ahead to request a vegetarian meal. Many families are happy to cook with seasonal vegetables or grains—especially if it means showcasing their garden.

8.4 Winery and Brewery Tours

Touring Croatia's Wine Country

Croatia's wine culture is both ancient and experimental. The Greeks brought vines to the Dalmatian coast over 2,500 years ago, and today that lineage survives in unique indigenous grapes like Plavac Mali, Pošip, and Malvazija Istarska. Wine here isn't just an accessory—it's part of daily life, poured with lunch, dinner, and celebration.

The best way to understand Croatian wine is to visit where it's made. In Istria, head for the hills around Motovun, Grožnjan, and

Momjan, where boutique estates offer tastings in medieval stone cellars or modern terraces overlooking vineyards. Many are family-run and invite guests to pair wines with local cheeses, truffle products, or homemade bread.

Dalmatia, particularly the Pelješac Peninsula, is Plavac Mali territory—bold reds that grow in rocky coastal soil with sweeping views of the Adriatic. Some of the most scenic wineries are tucked into slopes near Orebić, Potomje, and Dingač, accessible by winding roads best tackled slowly. Consider booking a tour with a driver if you want to sample freely.

Winery visits here are personal. You may be greeted by the winemaker's mother, walk the vineyard with a glass in hand, or end up staying for a multi-course lunch you didn't plan. That's part of the charm: hospitality is baked into the experience, and stories are as important as tannins.

Montenegro's Micro-Wineries

Montenegro is still emerging on the wine tourism map, but the experience can be just as rich—often with less polish and more heart. In the Crmnica Valley near Lake

Skadar, centuries-old vineyards produce bold reds and crisp whites. Some of the country's best small wineries are found here, many run by just a few people, often from the same family.

Most wineries are informal. You might be led into a stone cellar with low ceilings, where bottles are stacked in wooden crates and tastings are poured into mismatched glasses. That's not a flaw—it's a sign that what you're drinking was made with hands, not machines. Some producers don't even bottle everything; they sell by the liter, meant to be drunk young and often.

Places like Vukmirović Winery, Mrvaljević Estate, or Masnović Wines near Virpazar are known for welcoming travelers who show genuine interest. You may be offered house-made rakija, olives from the garden, or smoked ham sliced in front of you. While many producers speak only limited English, the language of wine and food is surprisingly universal.

The Craft Beer Scene

While wine reigns supreme, craft beer is gaining momentum, especially in Croatia. Cities like Zagreb, Split, and Rijeka now have a range of microbreweries and taprooms experimenting with IPAs, sours, and porters. Names like The Garden Brewery, Zmajska Pivovara, and Nova Runda are leading the charge. You'll also find beer festivals popping up in spring and summer, where local producers show off their seasonal brews.

Montenegro's scene is smaller but growing, centered around Podgorica and the coast. Look for labels like Montenegro Craft Brewery and Paun Pale Ale, often served at newer gastropubs and music bars. Don't expect massive selection, but the vibe is relaxed, the brews are getting better, and the interest from young locals is clear.

If you're into beer, check for seasonal events—like Split Beer Fest or Zagreb's Craft Beer Week—where you can sample from across the region and meet brewers in person.

Planning Tips for Tasting Tours

Wineries and breweries in the region tend to be small, personal, and sometimes rustic. Advance reservations are often necessary, especially outside major towns or during harvest. Don't rely on drop-ins, and don't expect a polished "tasting room" experience in the Napa sense. You're more likely to sit at someone's kitchen table than stand at a bar.

If you're driving, be aware that local laws for blood alcohol limits are strict—especially in Croatia (0.05% for most drivers, 0.00% for those under 24). Consider hiring a driver, joining a small-group tour, or simply spitting (which isn't rude in wine settings). Some guesthouses and agritourism sites offer overnight stays on-site, which turns a tasting into a full evening of eating, talking, and stargazing.

Chapter 9 – Where to Stay

Choosing the right place to stay can shape the entire feel of your trip—especially in Croatia and Montenegro, where accommodations range from centuries-old stone villas on the coast to tucked-away mountain lodges in national parks. This chapter breaks down the variety of lodging options available and gives you the context to choose wisely. Whether you're looking for urban convenience, rustic charm, or remote quiet, there's a lot to consider beyond price or star rating.

We'll explore how to match your accommodations with your travel goals—whether that's diving into a city's café scene, relaxing with a sea view, or waking up in the middle of nowhere with nothing but birdsong. From the practical (how to book and when) to the personal (what kind of traveler you are), this chapter is here to help you land somewhere that feels right—and maybe even memorable.

9.1 Choosing Hotels, Villas, Guesthouses

Hotels: From Business-Class to Boutique

Hotels in Croatia and Montenegro cover the full spectrum—from international chains and all-inclusive resorts to small family-run boutique hotels. In major cities like Zagreb, Split, and Podgorica, you'll find hotels tailored to business travelers with all the expected comforts: efficient service, good breakfast spreads, and quick access to transportation. These are great if you're passing through or want a no-fuss home base.

In historic towns like Dubrovnik, Kotor, and Trogir, hotel options tend to blend into the local architecture. Some occupy renovated palaces or stone houses with dramatic staircases, sea views, and heavy wooden doors that open onto quiet alleys. These hotels are often more expensive, but they put you right in the middle of things—and many offer genuinely personal service, like handwritten welcome notes and staff who know the bakery that opens earliest.

Be aware that star ratings don't always align with what you might expect elsewhere. A 4-star hotel in Montenegro, for example, might lack an elevator or offer a modest breakfast. In contrast, a 3-star guesthouse in Croatia might have a rooftop terrace and a host who brings you homemade liqueur on arrival. It pays to read between the lines—or better yet, between the reviews.

Villas and Holiday Homes

Renting a villa or holiday home is especially popular for groups, families, or anyone planning a slower-paced trip. In Istria, Dalmatia, and along the Bay of Kotor, you'll find countless private homes available for weekly rentals—some rustic and traditional, others sleek and modern with infinity pools overlooking the coast.

In Croatia, areas like Hvar, Korčula, Brač, and the Pelješac Peninsula are dotted with restored stone villas that balance privacy and convenience. Many are former family homes with thick walls, shaded terraces, and stone ovens still in working order. A good villa host will often arrange for grocery delivery, boat rentals, or a private cook if asked in advance.

Montenegro offers similar setups in places like Herceg Novi, Perast, or the hills above Budva, where terraced vineyards and mountain views are the norm. Inland regions like Durmitor or Plav also have cottage-style villas surrounded by wildflower meadows and endless trails—more suitable for nature lovers than partygoers.

If you're visiting during peak summer, book early—villas fill fast, especially those with sea views and easy beach access. In shoulder seasons (May–June, September–October), prices drop, and you may find better availability and friendlier cancellation terms.

Guesthouses and Family Stays

One of the best ways to feel at home in the Balkans is to stay in a guesthouse or sobe—a private room in a local's home, sometimes with breakfast and often with warm, unsolicited hospitality. This tradition goes back decades and remains one of the most affordable, authentic ways to stay.

You'll find sobes throughout both countries, especially in smaller towns and rural areas. Hosts often speak at least basic English or

German and will give you tips you won't find in any guidebook—like which beach is never crowded or who sells the best olive oil nearby. Some will treat you like family, offering homemade wine, fresh eggs, or a quick lesson in making šljivovica (plum brandy).

In Montenegro, mountain villages around Žabljak, Kolasin, and Cetinje have cozy lodgings run by families who double as hiking guides, cooks, or local historians. In Croatia, places like Ston, Mljet, or Motovun have excellent guesthouses in peaceful settings, often with long views across vineyards or down to the sea.

Guesthouses rarely have 24-hour reception, so plan to coordinate arrival times in advance. It's not uncommon for keys to be handed over by a neighbor or for your host's grandmother to do the check-in if you arrive before dinner. That's part of the charm.

9.2 Camping, Glamping & Eco-Lodges

Traditional Camping

Croatia and Montenegro are camper-friendly, especially along the coast, in the mountains, and near national parks. Campgrounds range from simple plots with shared bathrooms to full-service resorts with restaurants, pools, and rental bungalows. Croatia, in particular, has a long-established camping culture, especially among German, Dutch, and Slovenian visitors who drive down for the summer.

Along the Croatian Adriatic, you'll find many well-maintained campsites near Rovinj, Zadar, Pula, and the Makarska Riviera, often with shaded plots for tents, campervans, and caravans. Facilities are generally clean, and locations tend to be stunning—think pine forests leading directly to the sea. Some even offer private beach access or naturist areas (often marked as FKK).

Montenegro's camping scene is a bit more rugged and less regulated, but there are gems if you're willing to go off the beaten path. Sites near Lake Skadar, Durmitor National Park, and Biogradska Gora attract hikers, bikers, and road-trippers. Many are small family-run operations where the campsite is essentially part of the family farm—expect homemade cheese and jam at breakfast.

Wild camping is officially not permitted in most national parks or protected areas, though some travelers do it discreetly. If you're camping outside a designated site, be respectful of the land and locals, and always ask permission if you're near someone's property.

Glamping and Unusual Stays

If you like the idea of nature without sacrificing comfort, glamping options are growing—especially in Croatia. In Istria and Dalmatia, there are upscale tent lodges and eco-domes nestled in olive groves, vineyards, or by the sea. These usually come with proper beds, bathrooms, and sometimes even Wi-Fi and hot tubs. Think luxury meets landscape.

Popular spots include Arena One 99 Glamping near Pomer and Plitvice Holiday Resort, which offers treehouses, tipi-style tents, and lake bungalows close to the national park. In Montenegro, options are more limited but slowly expanding—look to Etno Selo Montenegro near Lake Skadar or the Eco Camp Katun in the Komovi Mountains for cozy wooden cabins with panoramic views.

These kinds of stays often appeal to couples, families, and anyone wanting something a little more immersive. They're not usually cheap, but if you're after quiet, stargazing, or privacy, they offer good value.

Eco-Lodges and Nature Retreats

Eco-tourism is growing steadily in both countries, especially in protected areas and rural villages looking to revive traditional lifestyles. Eco-lodges and retreats are typically off-grid or low-impact accommodations that focus on sustainability, local food, and slow living.

In Montenegro, the area around Plav, Gusinje, and Prokletije National Park has a handful of basic but comfortable ecolodges built in local styles—stone and timber, with wood-fired stoves and river views. Some are part of community-run tourism efforts, where income supports local families and conservation.

Croatia's inland areas, especially Lika and Zagorje, also have growing networks of eco-farms and retreats. These places often serve homegrown meals, host workshops (herbalism, foraging, traditional baking), and give you space to truly disconnect.

If you're interested in multi-day hiking, yoga retreats, or slow food travel, eco-lodges are worth exploring. You may trade modern amenities for peace, fresh air, and real connection—but for many travelers, that's exactly the point.

9.3 Insider Booking Tips & Peak-Season Strategies

Timing Is Everything

In the Adriatic, geometry matters—wildflowers bloom just before tourist trails overflow, and villa terraces fill fast come high summer. July and August stand out as tactic-free zones: if you haven't booked by March, most options—even moderately priced guesthouses—may already be taken or price-hiked. For the best window into authentic, uncrowded stays, aim for:

- Early May to late June: Cool mornings, quiet beaches, WILD lunches—especially during truffle season in Istria.

- September to early October: Warm seas, olive harvests, pastel sunsets and off-season restaurant menus—many open till mid-October.

- November–April: Ideal for low-season travelers—skiing in Durmitor, wine in Herceg Novi, city stays in Zagreb, but coastal villages will feel ghostly.

If you're set on summer, consider booking private apartments or villas early: there are dozens in Dalmatia and Montenegro that operate like timecapsules—light, sea-side, but fiercely loyal to past guests. Reach out directly, as owners listed on Airbnb or Vrbo often take returning guests off platform and offer a better experience.

Leverage Direct Connections

Small towns rely on word of mouth and return guests. Over-automation and platform dependency haven't reached every corner yet. Here's how to tap into that:

- Email or message hosts directly (WhatsApp's encryption makes it appealing): Ask if they have one or two extras "off the platform"—unused rooms or alternative apartments. Also, mention your travel style ("I love quiet evenings," etc.) and they'll nudge you subtly toward appropriate options.

- Join local travel groups: Facebook communities like "Croatia Travel Tips" or "Montenegro Backpackers" often share last-minute openings or hidden family-run rooms—a few euros cheaper than big sites.

- Connect with tourism offices in small towns—most maintain Excel sheets of pension-style accommodations not listed online. A quick call to Konavle, Žabljak, or Perast can turn up secret stays.

Map Your Way Around — Not All "Beachfront" Is Equal

Words like "beachfront" and "sea view" are everywhere—but dig deeper. The *type* of beach—and how easy it is to access—varies. In Croatia, sharp coastal elevation might mean "beachfront" involves steps or a drop into a bathing platform. In Montenegro, "seaside" villas may sit on cliff edges with rocky beaches below.

If you're booking, ask:

- *How do we get to the beach—steps, path, shuttle?*

- *Is parking private, public, free or paid daily?*

- *Is there air conditioning?* A stone-wall bedroom in Dubrovnik at noon without AC isn't charming—it's a sauna.

Unless you're relying on taxis, knowing the local bus schedule is also vital—many rural stops require walking 10–20 minutes from stations that don't notify you when a bus is coming or going.

Cancellation & Flexibility

Expect two broad categories:

1. Summer season/property with a platform: lots of restrictions, once-a-washer blocked deposit, measured cancellations.

2. Family-run/place-without-platform: casual, no-show means no stay without conversation—but very forgiving if you communicate clearly.

Pro tip: Book in pairs—make one fully refundable, reserve the other, and cancel whichever you don't need a week before.

For remote stays, ask about backup options if the unlikely happens (owner's elderly relative is hospitalized, neighbor can't host you). Most local guesthouses are small enough that a quick chat over the phone or through WhatsApp sorts it fast.

Pack for Check-In Surprises

Some guesthouses are guarded by Wi-Fi signal; others by grandmothers. Anticipate that you may arrive when "reception" is at lunch in a neighbor's kitchen.

- Recon the arrival: will your transport meet you? Confirm with the host.

- Expect simple: sometimes soap only, no shampoo; bring a micro-towel, portable outlet adapter (Euro plug), and a plug-in nightlight.

- If you have food restrictions, ask in advance. Olive oil—and accompanying bread—gets served like water. Great, but if you're gluten-intolerant or vegan, small mentions go a long way.

9.4 Family & Solo-Traveler Accommodations

Planning for Families

Traveling with toddlers or teens changes the requirements: stroller space, child-safe balconies, plug adapters you leave in, and breakfast schedules that align with early risers.

Choosing the Right Stay:

- An apartment or villa with separate bedroom/bathroom—common in Pelješac, Brač, Budva Old Town—allows privacy and flexibility.

- Short walk to beach: aim for ≤5 minutes and steps never more than 20; strollers hate cobbles.

- Kitchens are lifesavers: breakfast at 7 a.m. and pizza by 9 p.m.—especially useful for fussy eaters or freezing parents.

Activities Next Door:

- Look for stays near gentle beaches with shaded areas and playgrounds. Lošinj, Crikvenica, and Tivat are built for kids.

- Some properties offer toys, beach gear, or direct access to a garden. Ask if neighbors have kids; you might make a friendship by breakfast.

School-Inspired Stays:

- Guesthouses often offer mini cooking or craft lessons—painting olives, cheese-pressing, or rakija tasting for adults.

- Consider a buy-two-get-five discount offering child meals free at local konobas (some are family-run) if you stay for 3 nights or more.

Solo Travel: Good Stays That Connect

Going solo is freeing—but the right surroundings matter. Accommodations can make or break the experience.

Where to Stay:

- Central guesthouses in Split, Zagreb, or Kotor offer conversation and social mixing. Think shared terrace kitchens or courtyard breakfasts.

- Women-run homestays—especially around Istria's olive farms or Dubrovnik's islands—provide added trust and comfort. Hosts tend to be natural connectors, organizing dinners or book-sharing.

- Even private apartments often come with the host nearby—great for a chat

and going local.

Going Social:

- Options like Split's Hostel Split – The Downtown and Design Hostel include private rooms but with shared lounges and communal dinners, great for bumping into other solo travelers.

- Look for optional group cooking nights, wine-pairing events, or barbecue nights hosted by B&Bs—that way, you'll meet others organically.

Practical Confidence:

- Single travelers often feel more confident when staying on floors ≥2 with elevator, front desk hours, and options for shared laundry—places that feel "live-in" rather than a stranger's spare room.

- Wi-Fi is essential. Don't assume a countryside retreat will have reliable internet. If you need to work, ask beforehand or plan café backup.

Whether you're creating little childhood memories or seeking serendipity alone, the right lodging choice helps set the tone from the moment you step through the door. From host family dinners to city buzz or starlit solitude, accommodation in Croatia and Montenegro can be as memorable as the place itself.

Chapter 10 – On the Road: Itineraries

There's no single "best" way to explore Croatia and Montenegro. Every traveler arrives with different rhythms, interests, and time constraints—and this chapter helps you design a journey that suits all of them. Whether you're spending a week skimming the coastline, working your way inland, or mixing historical towns with outdoor adventure, the routes ahead give you grounded frameworks that can be adjusted to your pace. These aren't just dotted maps—they're real-world sequences that account for ferry timetables, border crossings, restaurant closing days, and the kind of off-the-path gems you only find by slowing down.

In the sections that follow, you'll find sample 7- and 10-day itineraries as well as flexible "pick-and-mix" modules for DIY trip builders and shorter themed escapes. We've accounted for travel logistics (like when not to rely on public transport), included local insights, and designed routes that don't rush you past the good stuff. Think of this as your launchpad—not just for where to go, but how to go in a way that aligns with how you actually want to travel.

10.1 Seven-Day Coastal Highlights

Who It's For

This route is built for travelers with limited time but big expectations—people who want to swim in the Adriatic, sip local wine, walk medieval streets, and still make room for one or two deeper experiences along the way. You'll move steadily south along the Croatian coast, starting in Split and ending in Kotor, Montenegro. It's linear, efficient, and heavy on seascapes, historic towns, and excellent meals with a view.

It's best done with a rental car or a combination of ferries and pre-booked transfers. If you're relying only on public transport, expect a slightly slower pace and fewer spontaneous detours.

Day 1: Split – Layers of Old and New

Split is more than just a ferry port. Spend your first day not rushing onto a boat, but easing into Croatia by exploring Diocletian's Palace, a living Roman ruin that still houses shops, apartments, and wine bars. Visit the green market in the morning for fresh figs and sheep's cheese, take a late afternoon dip at Bačvice or Kasjuni Beach, then climb Marjan Hill for sunset. For dinner, head to a konoba in Varoš for slow-roasted lamb or seafood risotto.

Optional add-on: If you arrive early, consider a half-day trip to Trogir—only 30 minutes away but a world apart, with a walkable historic core surrounded by sea.

Day 2–3: Hvar – Lavender, Fortresses, and Wine

Hop on a morning catamaran or ferry to Hvar. The town gets busy in peak summer, but if you time it right (late spring or early autumn), you'll find a relaxed pace and plenty of beauty. Stay in Hvar Town for nightlife and energy, or opt for Stari Grad for a quieter, more local feel. On Day 2, climb to the Spanish Fortress for sweeping views, and wander through cobbled alleys of the port.

Spend Day 3 wine tasting in the interior, biking past lavender fields (if in season), or exploring the Pakleni Islands by kayak or taxi boat.

Day 4: Korčula – Walled Charm

From Hvar, catch a ferry to Korčula. The island's namesake town often gets called "Little Dubrovnik" for its honey-colored walls and red-roof skyline, but it's got its own distinct feel. It's less theatrical, more intimate. Explore its narrow lanes, enjoy a seafood lunch overlooking the Pelješac Channel, and if you're lucky, catch a Moreška sword dance performance. Rent bikes and pedal through the vineyards around Lumbarda in the late afternoon.

Stay overnight—Korčula has a calm charm once day-trippers leave.

Day 5: Pelješac Peninsula – Wine, Oysters, and Solitude

In the morning, take a short ferry to Orebić and pick up a rental car if you haven't already. Drive the Pelješac Peninsula slowly—stop at family-owned wineries like Grgić or Matuško for robust Dingač reds, and detour to Ston for its enormous defensive walls and salt pans. Don't miss a lunch of fresh oysters and mussels, pulled straight from the bay.

Spend the night in or near Ston—or, if you're having a good time, continue south to Dubrovnik and stay on the quieter Lapad peninsula.

Day 6: Dubrovnik – Beyond the Crowds

Dubrovnik deserves a full day, but how you spend it makes all the difference. Arrive early to walk the walls before cruise crowds arrive, then retreat to quieter corners like the Buža bar (cliffside drinks and sea views) or the Franciscan Monastery's pharmacy museum. Take a late boat to Lokrum Island if the weather's clear—or escape uphill to the village of Gornji Kono for lunch above the fray.

Sunset from Mt. Srđ, reached by cable car or footpath, closes the day in cinematic style.

Day 7: Bay of Kotor – Montenegro's Fjord

Cross into Montenegro in the morning—it's just a two-hour drive to Kotor, though border delays can add time. The Bay of Kotor feels like a mountain-wrapped mirror. Park the car and wander the fortified town, stopping for grilled calamari or black risotto. For a deeper finale, climb the fortress trail above town or take a boat ride to Our Lady of the Rocks.

Stay overnight if possible. Kotor is ethereal after dark, once the sun sets behind the peaks and the day trippers disappear.

10.2 Ten-Day Croatia + Montenegro Journey

Who It's For

If you've got 10 days and want to weave together the best of both countries, this itinerary offers a balanced blend of cities, coast, islands, and inland charm. It's designed for travelers who want to see the big names—Dubrovnik, Kotor, Split—but also tuck into lesser-visited gems like Perast, the Cetina River Valley, or the wine country of Pelješac. This trip is best done with a car for flexibility, but it can be modified for bus/train/ferry travel with some planning.

This is a rich and full itinerary, but with enough room to breathe.

Days 1–2: Zagreb to Plitvice

Start in Zagreb, Croatia's capital. Its café culture, Austro-Hungarian buildings, and compact museums offer a gentle start. After a day exploring the Upper Town, take a morning drive or bus to Plitvice Lakes National Park, arriving early enough to walk the wooden trails and boardwalks before crowds hit. Stay nearby in a guesthouse to soak in the quiet forest air overnight.

Days 3–4: Split & Krka

Head south to Split, stopping at Krka National Park en route if waterfalls call. In Split, spend time in Diocletian's Palace, wander the Riva, and explore Marjan's piney trails. If you're up for it, detour to Klis Fortress or Salona, the Roman ruins nearby.

Days 5–6: Hvar or Brač

Pick one island. Hvar for its mix of glamour and nature; Brač for laid-back beaches and the famous Zlatni Rat spit in Bol. Either way, book ferries in advance. In Hvar, you can wine-taste or island-hop. In Brač, rent scooters to find secluded coves and stone-carving heritage.

Days 7–8: Korčula & Pelješac

Spend a full day on Korčula, soaking in the Venetian-style charm, then ferry to Orebić and drive the Pelješac Peninsula. Visit Ston, sample oysters, and follow the wine road through the hills. Stay overnight at a vineyard estate or simple seaside inn.

Days 9–10: Dubrovnik & Kotor

Wrap the trip with Dubrovnik and Kotor, using your final days to explore both cities slowly. Don't try to do too much—pick a few corners of each. In Dubrovnik, consider a kayak trip around the city walls. In Kotor, rent bikes or walk the Bay shoreline. Cross the border with time to spare, and enjoy the shift in atmosphere as you move from Croatia's marble squares to Montenegro's moody mountains.

10.3 Build-Your-Own Adventure: Pick & Mix

Not every trip fits neatly into a week or ten-day window, and not every traveler wants to follow someone else's path. Maybe you're here for slow travel, or maybe you're hopping between flights and ferry docks with only three days to spare. This section is for those who want to build their own trip—selecting locations, experiences, and pacing that match their interests rather than a prewritten schedule.

What follows isn't a list of destinations—it's a curated set of building blocks. You can mix and match coastal towns with inland nature, alternate historic cities with beach time, or pair wine regions with active adventures. Each module below includes travel context, realistic timing, and how it fits into a broader route. Think of it as a practical menu for shaping your own itinerary.

Coastal Basecamps (2–4 nights each)

Split, Dubrovnik, Kotor, and Hvar Town all make great bases for exploring wider regions. Split connects easily to Trogir, Šibenik, and Krka National Park. Dubrovnik pairs with Lokrum, Cavtat, or Pelješac. Hvar Town offers access to the Pakleni Islands, Stari Grad, and inland wineries. Kotor is a launchpad for Perast, Lovćen National Park, and the Vrmac ridge.

Stay in one of these hubs for 2–4 nights, take day trips by ferry, car, or foot, and return each night to the same bed—ideal for travelers who want a mix of activity and downtime.

Wine & Food Routes

If food and drink shape your travels, consider these modules:

- Pelješac Peninsula (2 days) for oysters in Mali Ston and full-bodied

Dingač reds.

- Istria (3–4 days) for truffle hunting, olive oil tastings, and hill towns like Motovun and Grožnjan.

- Central Montenegro (2–3 days) around Lake Skadar, where family-run wineries and rustic taverns pair local Vranac wines with river fish or slow-roasted meats.

These regions are best explored with a car and some flexibility. Many of the best meals are found at rural konobas, where you may need to call ahead or wait a while. But that's part of the point.

Islands and Ferries

Croatia's ferry network makes island-hopping feasible if you understand the timing. For example:

- Hvar–Korčula–Mljet works well west to east.

- Brač–Hvar can work too, but not always directly.

- Mljet is best done as a full-day trip or overnight from Dubrovnik or Korčula.

Check ferry routes early and plan at least two nights per island to avoid travel fatigue. A tip: don't over-island. Choose two islands max unless you have more than ten days.

Nature and Inland Options

For hikes, rivers, and mountains, use these as flexible add-ons:

- **Plitvice Lakes (1–2 days):** Best on the way from Zagreb to the coast. Avoid weekends and arrive early.

- **Durmitor National Park (2–3 days):** Great for summer hiking, rafting, and cool mountain air.

- **Cetinje–Lovćen–Njeguši loop (1–2 days):** Combines history, scenery, and food in Montenegro's spiritual heart.

- **Cetina River Valley near Omiš:** A half- or full-day rafting or canyoning detour from Split.

These modules balance out the historic towns and coastline with a breath of fresh air and fewer crowds.

Combine by Theme or Mood

You might string together three "slow travel" bases (Korčula, Kotor, Stari Grad) and spend a few days in each. Or do a wine-heavy arc (Zagreb → Istria → Pelješac → Lake Skadar). Or maybe you want nothing but national parks and outdoor time. The real key is pacing: don't try to do too much. These countries reward those who linger.

10.4 Short Breaks and Thematic Routes

Not everyone is coming for two weeks. Maybe you're tacking a few days onto a work trip, sailing in for a long weekend, or just making a targeted escape. This section offers short, intentional routes that hit specific interests—ideal for travelers who want to focus on one region or theme and get the most out of it without spreading too thin.

Each route below can be done in 3–5 days, depending on travel time and energy level. They're also good options for returning travelers who've seen the highlights and want to dive deeper into something specific.

For History Buffs: Dalmatian Time Travel

Base in Split for Roman ruins, detour to Salona and Klis Fortress, then ferry to Trogir and Šibenik, both medieval gems. End with a night in Zadar, where Roman roads meet sea organs and postmodern light shows.

Optional add-on: overnight in Nin, one of Croatia's oldest towns, with a tiny 9th-century church and long stretches of quiet beach.

For Nature Lovers: Parks and Peaks

Fly into Zagreb or Dubrovnik, then head to Plitvice Lakes, Paklenica, or Durmitor depending on your base. Montenegro's

Biogradska Gora is great for those wanting a less-touristed version of Durmitor with ancient forest walks. In Croatia, Velebit offers wild hiking and striking limestone terrain.

These routes are especially good in shoulder seasons (May/June or September), when trails are open but not packed.

For Wine and Food Travelers: Inland Istria or Lake Skadar

Inland Istria is ideal for a relaxed long weekend: stay in Motovun or Grožnjan, drive between hill towns, stop at wineries and truffle farms, and end the day in a stone courtyard with a glass of Malvazija.

Lake Skadar in Montenegro is a more rustic, riverine version. Based in Virpazar or Rijeka Crnojevića, explore the lake by boat, taste local Vranac wines, and hike or cycle between villages. Both routes offer deep regional flavor in just a few days.

For Sea-Lovers: Island Mini Loops

If you've already seen Split and Dubrovnik, try this:

- Brač → Hvar → Korčula in 4–5 days
- Or, for something quieter: Šolta → Vis

These work best with pre-booked ferries and light luggage. Travel between islands early in the day so you're not rushing meals or sunset swims. Stay two nights per island and give yourself time to walk, swim, and wander.

For The Romantics: Bay of Kotor Slow Burn

Spend 3–4 nights in Perast, Dobrota, or Prčanj—smaller villages on the Bay of Kotor. Rent bikes or paddleboards, take a boat to Our Lady of the Rocks, and wander through baroque palaces turned into boutique hotels or small museums. If you're feeling ambitious, hike up to the fortress above Kotor before dawn and watch the fog lift over the bay.

It's not about hitting every site—it's about giving yourself space to absorb the atmosphere.

Chapter 11 – Safety, Health & Practical Advice

Traveling through Croatia and Montenegro is generally smooth, safe, and welcoming, but knowing how to navigate local systems—roads, ferries, healthcare, or even social norms—can make the difference between a relaxed trip and one filled with unnecessary stress. This chapter focuses on what travelers really need to know to stay safe, travel responsibly, and handle surprises with minimal fuss.

From common-sense street smarts to practical guidance on mountain trails, border crossings, and ferry timetables, this section blends cultural insight with concrete tips. You'll also find help for understanding local etiquette, traffic laws, emergency contacts, and what to do if you lose your passport or need a doctor on a Sunday. It's not the most glamorous part of trip planning, but it might be the one that keeps your plans on track when something doesn't go as expected.

11.1 Staying Safe in Cities and Nature

Urban Street Sense

Croatia and Montenegro are among the safest countries in Europe, but everyday precautions still go a long way—especially in tourist-heavy areas. In busy squares like Split's Riva, Dubrovnik's Stradun, and Kotor's Old Town, pickpockets look for distractions. To stay safe:

- Choose secure bags: Cross-body bags with zippers, or money belts inside jackets.

- Carry photocopies: Keep a paper copy of your passport, visas, and key documents, separate from the originals.

- Avoid late-night isolation: Most incidents happen away from well-lit, crowded spots. Stick to lively streets if you're out late.

The police generally respond quickly in tourist areas. If you ever feel unwell, lost, or unsafe, don't hesitate to approach officers—many speak basic English and are used to helping travelers.

Stranger Danger vs. Genuine Hospitality

One of the best things about traveling here is how approachable locals are. Whether you're asking for directions, sampling wine, or stopping your car to admire a view, you'll often be met with genuine kindness. Most Montenegrins and Croatians enjoy meeting visitors and offering tips, but always remember:

- If someone offers unsolicited or persistent help, especially drivers offering rides, politely decline and walk away.

- If you're invited somewhere unfamiliar, verify details with your host or hotel contact.

- Accept free invitations like drinks or snacks—but if something feels off, follow your instincts.

Hiking and Mountain Safety

The inland areas—from Croatia's Karst regions to Montenegro's alpine terrain—are beautiful, but can be dangerous if unprepared.

1. Know your loop: Many trails aren't clearly signed. Use GPS, carry a printed local map, and ask your accommodation host for trail conditions.

2. Stay weather-aware: Mountain weather changes fast. An afternoon storm in Durmitor can shift from steady drizzle to lightning in an hour.

3. Hike smart: Bring trail snacks, warm layers, a hat—even in summer. In remote areas, a basic first-aid kit and a whistle can make a huge difference.

During summer, some trails are littered with broken glass from careless visitors. Enjoy the views, but watch your footing and avoid cliff edges where warning signs haven't been posted.

At Sea and on Coves

The Adriatic coast is a cornerstone of the experience, but it demands respect:

- Know your beach type. Croatia's coast varies from sandy coves to rocky ledges, forest access to cliff-drops.

- Swim with caution:

    - Watch for local warnings or flags—red for strong currents, blue for calm water.

    - Rent sea shoes if stepping into rocky waters—avoid sea urchin spines.

    - Paddleboard or kayak in calmer morning seas before coastal breezes pick up.

Self-drive boats are increasingly popular, but not without risk:

- Make sure the operator provides life jackets, a radio, and emergency instructions.

- Know the basics: pay attention to navigation lanes, offshore platforms, and mooring zones.

- While alcohol and driving don't share season passes, enforcement varies—stay sober.

Rural Risks and Hidden Hazards

Away from cities, different safety issues arise:

- Wildlife:

    - Wild boars move in packs, mostly at dusk — leave them alone and backtrack slowly if spotted.

    - Snake bites are rare but possible—wear sturdy shoes and avoid tall grass by trail edges.

- Ticks: Common in forests from spring to autumn. Check skin/clothing after each hike and use insect repellent containing DEET or picaridin.

- Livestock: Don't assume dogs or herds will keep to themselves on farm roads or mountain paths. Slow down and give them space.

11.2 Getting Around: Driving Rules, Ferries

Cars, Roads & Cross-Border Driving

Renting a car is one of the easiest ways to explore at your own pace, but the key is preparation:

- International Driving Permit (IDP): Most rental agencies require an IDP in addition to your driver's license.

- Insurance:
    - Standard CDW (collision damage waiver) typically excludes animals,

undercarriage, and windscreen—but can be upgraded.

- If crossing into Montenegro or Bosnia, request an international "Green Card" before departure to avoid border fines.

Croatian vs. Montenegrin Road Conditions

Croatia's main motorways (A1, A6) and coastal roads are well maintained. Expect scenic but sometimes slow movement in summer congestion. Watch for livestock or tourist buses on two-lane coastal roads.

In Montenegro, highland roads near Durmitor, Lovćen, and Tara Canyon may be narrow with tight hairpin bends. Some gothic mountain tunnels lack lighting—set headlights early. Watch for:

- Unexpected speed bumps in towns;

- Lack of shoulder space;

- Occasional stopped tractors or sheep flocks.

Always obey posted speed limits—cameras monitor roads around tunnels and urban zones. Fines are issued on-site to foreigners and often require payment then and there.

Border Crossings

Croatia and Montenegro share a land border with passport checks—prepare for short waits, especially during peak summer days.

- Passports are required, even for EU citizens—most checkpoints don't accept ID cards.

- Borders are quiet overnight but busy during daytime; plan shifts or breakfast breaks before moving.

Suppose you're taking a private transfer or bus—double-check your operator's validity and routing, especially if they use the Neum Corridor in Bosnia, which still requires border stops for two countries in one short stretch.

Ferry Logistics and Island Travel

Jadrolinija, Krilo, and Kapetan Luka provide Croatia's primary ferry network. Here's how to navigate them effectively:

- Car vs. passenger ferries: Cars take longer, operate less frequently, but arrive regardless of luggage restrictions. Catamarans are faster and more convenient if you travel light.

- Reservations:

    - Cars: Almost mandatory from July to early September.

    - Walk-on passengers: Consider booking for Hvar, Korčula, and Vis for midday departures.

- Timetables vary seasonally—check schedules on local tourism sites and confirm departure time the day before. Croatian fährpläne usually shifts near October 1.

- Loading/unloading may feel chaotic—queue early, ask

dockworkers, and follow lanes carefully.

Montenegro has no island ferries but does operate water taxis in Kotor and boat services to destinations like Our Lady of the Rocks or Lustica Bay. These are convenient, often comparable in cost to land taxis, and run more frequently during summer.

Public Transport: Buses, Trains & Minibuses

Croatian city transit is generally reliable. Zagreb, Osijek, Pula, Split, and Dubrovnik have bus or tram networks. Split's city bus is useful between the center and Marjan Hill. Keep small change; tickets can be sold onboard or at kiosks.

Intercity buses run frequently: check schedules for Split–Dubrovnik (~4 hrs with border) and Dubrovnik–Kotor (~2–3 hrs including border). Expect occasional delays due to roadworks.

In Montenegro, "combis" (shared minivans) connect villages with larger towns. They can be efficient, but your stop may be communicated verbally to the driver. Avoid rides after dark on remote roads.

Cycling, Scooter & Boat Rentals

Bikes and scooters are popular, with rentals common in cities and major tourist hubs. Keep in mind:

- Helmet laws: Some towns require helmets and reflective vests at night—but enforcement is lax.

- Scooter pitfalls: Road surfaces vary; narrow, windy roads make scooters trickier outside urban areas—cars may not give you clearance.

- Boat hires: Require boater licenses for larger engines. Always confirm they'll provide life jackets, flares, and safety briefings. For cliffs or strong winds, leave the rental undisturbed.

11.3 Health, Insurance & Emergencies

What to Know Before You Go

Croatia and Montenegro both have functioning healthcare systems that are accessible to tourists, but they operate a bit differently than in North America or Western Europe. While Croatia is an EU member, Montenegro is not, which can impact coverage if you rely solely on European Health Insurance Cards (EHICs). Either way, travel insurance is highly recommended—not just for peace of mind but to ensure you're not stuck with large out-of-pocket expenses in case of illness, injury, or evacuation.

Comprehensive travel insurance should cover:

- Emergency medical care (including transport)

- Trip interruption or delay

- Coverage for activities like hiking, boating, or diving

- Repatriation in case of severe illness

It's also wise to check if your plan covers pre-existing conditions or dental care, and if private clinic access is included—particularly in Montenegro, where public facilities can be underfunded or understaffed.

Pharmacies, Clinics & What to Expect

In both countries, pharmacies (apotekas in Croatia, apoteke in Montenegro) are widespread, including in small coastal towns. Many are open late, and some larger cities have 24/7 emergency pharmacies.

- Common medications such as painkillers, allergy meds, or antibiotics are typically available over the counter or with a quick consultation.

- Bring a printed list of medications, ideally with the generic (not brand) names and dosage, since some Western brands may not be available.

- If you wear glasses or contact lenses, carry a spare pair and your prescription—optometrists can be found in most city centers, but they may not stock your specific lenses.

For minor injuries or illness, walk-in clinics are usually accessible and affordable. In tourist zones, especially in Croatia, staff often speak English, German, or Italian.

Emergency Numbers and Local Support

- 112 is the universal emergency number in both countries. It connects you to ambulance, fire, and police services.

- In Croatia, the Red Cross also offers traveler assistance at some locations, especially during peak summer months.

- Most larger hotels can arrange a doctor visit to your room (often at an extra fee).

- For urgent needs in rural areas, especially in Montenegro's interior, dial 124 for ambulance service, though response times can vary.

If you're staying off-grid—say, in a glamping site, a mountain hut, or a small island village—it's smart to know where the nearest clinic or medical center is. Reception staff, local hosts, or guesthouse owners are often your first point of contact in case of emergency.

Food Safety and Water

Tap water is safe to drink throughout both countries, unless otherwise noted (some very remote or old village systems may have signage advising against it). Restaurants and food stalls generally follow decent hygiene standards, but a few precautions help:

- Avoid unpeeled fruit or raw seafood from street stalls.
- Wash your hands before meals—many public toilets lack soap, so pack hand sanitizer.

Stomach bugs are rare but can happen, especially in high summer. Keep oral rehydration salts in your travel kit just in case.

Mental and Emotional Well-Being

Traveling can be stressful, even on vacation. If you're feeling overwhelmed—especially if traveling solo or off-season—don't hesitate to slow down and ask for help. Locals are often warm and willing to assist.

For deeper mental health support:

- Croatia has several English-speaking therapists in Zagreb, Split, and Rijeka, though access may require private payment.

- Montenegro has fewer options, but embassies or expat forums (like those in Kotor or Budva) can sometimes connect you with resources.

If you need emergency mental health assistance, call 112 and explain your situation—operators can connect you to local hospitals or help lines.

11.4 Locals' Etiquette and Cultural Norms

A Culture of Hospitality

Both Croatians and Montenegrins pride themselves on being warm and generous hosts. While each region has its own nuance, there are some unspoken rules that help visitors show respect and get a more authentic experience.

- Greetings matter: A firm handshake and eye contact are expected when meeting someone new, even casually.

- If you're invited to someone's home, bring a small gift—wine, chocolate, or flowers are common choices.

- Always take your shoes off at the door unless your host tells you otherwise.

Hospitality isn't just formal—it's social currency. You may be offered coffee, food, or even homemade rakija (fruit brandy) within minutes of meeting someone. Declining is okay but should be done politely; saying something like "maybe later" or "thank you, but I just ate" softens the refusal.

Gender, Age, and Social Hierarchies

Respect for elders is culturally ingrained, especially in rural areas and traditional households. If you're speaking to an older local, it's courteous to use formal greetings and allow them to initiate more casual language.

In general:

- Gender roles are still somewhat traditional, especially in rural Montenegro. That said, women travelers—solo or not—are welcomed and generally treated with respect.

- LGBTQ+ travelers are more accepted in urban Croatia (especially Zagreb and Split), though visibility in smaller towns may still draw attention. Montenegro is slowly shifting toward more tolerance, but discretion is advised outside of coastal cities like Budva.

Dining & Social Manners

Meals are seen as social rituals, not just fuel. Whether you're in a konoba (traditional tavern) or a seaside restaurant:

- Don't rush. Meals can take several hours—especially if you're sharing grilled fish or lamb pika.

- Wait for the host to start eating, especially at family or group gatherings.

- Tipping is customary but not obligatory. Rounding up or leaving 10% is standard in most restaurants.

At cafes, you're welcome to linger. Coffee culture is strong, especially in Croatia, where locals often spend hours chatting over a macchiato or bijela kava (milk coffee). Don't expect quick service—relax and join the rhythm.

Language and Communication

Most young people speak English, especially in cities and coastal areas. In rural Montenegro or inland Croatia, older generations may not—but will try to help regardless.

- Learn a few local words: "Hvala" (thank you), "Dobar dan" (good day), and "Molim" (please) go a long way.

- Locals appreciate effort. Even if your pronunciation is rough, attempting a few phrases builds good will.

- Don't shout or get impatient—raising your voice, especially at service workers or officials, is seen as deeply rude.

Religious & Cultural Sensitivity

- Croatia is predominantly Catholic, while Montenegro is more mixed—Eastern Orthodox, Muslim, and Catholic traditions overlap. Respect is expected at churches, monasteries, and mosques.

- Dress modestly when visiting religious sites—cover shoulders, skip shorts, and remove hats.

- On religious holidays (like Easter, Assumption Day, or Orthodox Christmas), some services may be limited, and towns may be quieter than usual.

Photographing locals without permission, especially in remote or religious areas, is frowned upon. A friendly gesture and pointing to your camera is usually enough to ask permission nonverbally.

Final Thoughts

Understanding the culture is more than just being polite—it's how you unlock richer experiences. From casual coffees and shared glasses of rakija to navigating a health clinic or showing respect in a monastery, these small gestures add up. Travel, after all, is not just about seeing places but being part of them, even briefly.

Chapter 12 – Seasonal Insights & Packing

Planning a trip to Croatia or Montenegro means thinking in layers—literally and figuratively. The Adriatic coast and the Dinaric Alps share the same region but operate on entirely different climates. One morning you might be basking on a sunny island beach, and by evening, pulling on a fleece in a mountain village. This chapter helps you prepare for that kind of variety. Whether you're hiking in Durmitor, strolling Dubrovnik's polished stone lanes, or attending a music festival in Split, you'll want to pack smart—not just light.

This section breaks down seasonal quirks, cultural dress codes, and packing essentials. You'll find real-world advice for travelers who want to look respectful, stay comfortable, and avoid common missteps. We'll talk through the difference between festival fashion and monastery modesty, unpack what "off-season" really means in the Balkans, and offer gear suggestions that are both practical and kind to the landscapes you'll be exploring.

12.1 Packing for Seaside & Mountain

Climate Contrasts and Why They Matter

Packing for the Balkans is more complicated than it seems. On paper, Croatia and Montenegro both enjoy a Mediterranean climate along the coast—hot, dry summers and mild winters. But that's only part of the story. Inland and at higher elevations, things change fast. Montenegro's mountains and Croatia's national parks like Plitvice and Paklenica can be ten to fifteen degrees cooler than coastal towns on the same day. Wind, rain, and even snow are possible deep into spring and early autumn.

So if your trip includes both sea and hill—say, Kotor and Lovćen, or Dubrovnik and the Konavle highlands—you'll need to be ready for quick shifts in temperature and terrain.

Smart Layers, Not Just Warm Clothes

Instead of packing "for the cold" or "for the heat," think in layers. A light base layer (t-shirt or tank), mid-layer (long-sleeve shirt or fleece), and an outer shell (light jacket or windbreaker) can be mixed and matched depending on where you are and what you're doing. Mountain mornings can be brisk even in July, while ferry decks can be windy year-round.

If you're doing any hiking—especially in Biogradska Gora, Durmitor, or northern Velebit—add:

- A waterproof jacket or poncho
- Breathable, sweat-wicking shirts
- Durable trail shoes with grip (wet limestone is slippery)

Coastal Comfort Without the Clunk

On the coast, especially in summer, days are long and hot, and the UV index is high. Lightweight, breathable clothing will be your best friend. Linen shirts, cotton dresses, quick-dry shorts, and wide-brim hats are ideal. That said, coastal breezes can pick up quickly in the evenings. A light wrap or sweater is worth the space in your daypack.

Sun protection is key. Locals usually hit the beach early or late in the day, avoiding the 11am–3pm window when sunburns happen fastest. Pack reef-safe sunscreen, polarized sunglasses, and a refillable water bottle. Croatia has plenty of natural shade on its beaches (especially those with pine trees), but Montenegro's coastal stretches can be more exposed.

Swimwear is casual, but topless sunbathing is rare outside of specific beaches (often marked as naturist or FKK). Bring more than one swimsuit—they take a while to dry in humid seaside towns.

Footwear: Don't Underestimate the Pavement

Croatian and Montenegrin streets often mean stone—uneven, polished, and sometimes steep. That goes double for Old Towns like Split, Trogir, Kotor, and Herceg Novi. Leave flimsy sandals at home. Opt for sturdy walking shoes or sandals with grip, especially if you're planning full days of sightseeing or market-hopping.

For mountain regions, proper hiking boots are a must. Some routes in Montenegro's interior cross shale, scree, or loose gravel. Even well-trodden trails like the Ladder of Kotor can challenge balance and ankle strength if you're not wearing supportive shoes.

Off-Season and Shoulder Travel

Visiting outside of summer? October through April can bring rain, especially along the Dalmatian coast. Pack a compact umbrella or rain jacket, along with shoes that can handle wet cobblestones. Winter in the Balkans can be surprisingly cold inland. Central heating is common in cities but less so in rural areas or older apartments. A thermal layer or two can make chilly mornings more bearable.

A Note on Laundry

If you're traveling longer than a week, consider packing fewer outfits and planning to do laundry mid-trip. Most larger cities and tourist hubs have laundromats or drop-off services. In rural guesthouses, asking to wash a few things by hand is usually fine—just be polite and offer to compensate. Quick-dry fabrics make it easier to do a rinse-and-wear routine without waiting a full day for clothes to dry.

12.2 Dressing for Festivals and Culture

What to Wear When Everyone's Looking

Festivals in Croatia and Montenegro run the gamut—from classical music in Dubrovnik to EDM in Budva, folklore parades in Sinj to indie film screenings in Kotor. The vibe can shift dramatically depending on the venue, the town, and the crowd. But there's one consistent thread: people show up. Dressing like you just left the beach is fine if you're at a beach club, but it may feel out of place in a historical theater or old city square.

At music festivals, you'll see everything from relaxed linen fits to full-on sparkle. Just keep in mind that many events are held outdoors in stony plazas or along harbors, where you'll be on your feet. Opt for comfortable but stylish footwear, something that can handle both cobblestones and spilled wine.

For cultural festivals—especially folk events, religious processions, or classical concerts—go with respectful, semi-casual clothing. A button-down, maxi dress, or jumpsuit works well. Shorts are fine for most settings, but avoid very short or tight options if you're attending anything religious or traditional.

Visiting Churches, Monasteries, and Mosques

Both countries have deep religious traditions. Croatia is predominantly Catholic, while Montenegro blends Orthodox Christianity with Islam in some regions. Modest dress is essential when visiting sacred sites:

- Cover shoulders and knees

- Avoid low-cut tops or sheer clothing

- Carry a scarf or shawl—it's an easy way to adapt quickly

Some sites (like Ostrog Monastery or the Franciscan Monastery in Dubrovnik) may offer wraparound skirts or shawls at the entrance. But don't count on it—better to have your own.

Men should remove hats and avoid sleeveless tops. Women may be expected to cover their heads in Orthodox or Islamic sites, especially outside major cities.

How Locals Dress—and How That Affects You

In urban Croatia—especially Zagreb, Split, and Rijeka—you'll notice locals dress neatly. Even casual wear is well-fitted and coordinated. Montenegro's coastal cities, particularly Kotor and Budva, have a beachier aesthetic, but you'll still see locals putting effort into their appearance in the evenings. Flip-flops and workout clothes may stand out unless you're near a beach or hiking trail.

Wearing appropriate, respectful clothing won't just help you blend in—it often affects the way you're treated. It can lead to better service in restaurants, more positive attention in shops, and warmer interactions with locals.

Temperature vs. Dress Code

It might be 35°C in Dubrovnik in July, but that doesn't mean anything goes. In many town centers, especially historic ones, you'll find a mix of tourists in tank tops and locals in lightweight long sleeves. Dress for the weather, but keep in mind the context—especially if you're dining out, attending a performance, or walking through a local neighborhood.

Montenegrin mountain towns like Žabljak or Plav can still be chilly at night in summer, so bring a warm layer if you're planning an evening concert or open-air dinner.

Festival Bags and Practical Add-ons

Many festivals limit bag size for security. A compact daypack or crossbody bag works best. Bring:

- A reusable water bottle

- A scarf or sarong (multi-use for sun, wind, or coverage)

- Small flashlight or headlamp (especially in rural settings or after outdoor concerts)

Leave valuables at home—especially large cameras, bulky wallets, or designer bags. Petty theft is rare but possible in crowded areas.

12.3 Seasonal Pros/Cons: Off-Season Tips

Timing Matters—More Than You Think

When to visit Croatia and Montenegro isn't just a question of weather—it's about rhythm. These countries operate on distinct seasonal cadences, and knowing how the months shape the local experience can make or break your trip. Summer might seem like the obvious choice, but it comes with crowds, heat, and higher prices. Spring and autumn offer a more relaxed vibe, while winter strips everything back to its essentials—quiet towns, low-key hiking, and cultural introspection.

There's no single "best" time to go. But each season brings trade-offs that are worth considering, depending on your priorities: sunbathing vs. hiking, nightlife vs. solitude, sightseeing vs. swimming.

Summer (June to August): Beauty, Buzz, and Big Crowds

This is peak season—when the Adriatic coast is alive with tourists, festivals, and long beach days. You'll find buzzing harbors, packed ferries, and nightlife that goes until dawn. It's also when prices hit their highest point, and accommodations in popular towns like Dubrovnik, Hvar, or Budva often need to be booked months in advance.

The pros: warm sea, reliable sunshine, cultural festivals, and nonstop energy.

The cons: large cruise crowds (especially in Split and Dubrovnik), inflated costs, parking headaches, and sometimes exhausting heat. Inland towns can feel sleepy, as many locals head to the coast for seasonal work.

Shoulder Season (Late April to May, September to mid-October): The Local Favorite

Locals and seasoned travelers often agree—this is the sweet spot. In spring, wildflowers and greenery transform the inland landscapes, and national parks like Plitvice and Durmitor are stunning without the summer crush. Early autumn offers warm seas, soft sunsets, and wine harvests in full swing.

Transportation is still frequent, but not overcrowded. You'll have space to breathe, prices begin to dip, and locals have more time for conversation. It's a great season for photographers, hikers, and anyone hoping to blend cultural sightseeing with outdoor exploration.

That said, some ferries and seasonal routes begin reducing service in late October. Check local timetables if your itinerary depends on smaller island connections or mountain roads.

Off-Season (November to March): Solitude and Slow Travel

This is the least-traveled window—but not without its charm. The coast quiets down dramatically, especially in smaller seaside towns like Korčula, Cavtat, or Petrovac. Some restaurants, hotels, and ferry routes shut down altogether. But inland cities—Zagreb, Podgorica, Cetinje, and even Split—carry on with daily life, often hosting cozy Christmas markets or cultural events.

It's a great time for low-key travel. If you're after museum visits, urban cafes, or snowshoeing in Montenegro's mountains, you'll find peace and low prices. But you'll need to be more self-sufficient—many services run on shorter hours, and weather can be wet or cold, especially in the north.

Region-by-Region Considerations

- The Dalmatian Coast: Packed in summer, dreamy in shoulder season, ghostly quiet in winter. Many coastal towns are deeply seasonal.

- The Islands: Ferry service slows down after October and may be suspended altogether in rough weather. Hvar, Brač, and Korčula are best visited between May and September.

- **Montenegrin Mountains:** Ideal for hiking May–October. Winter brings snow sports, but conditions can be unpredictable. Towns like Žabljak are mostly closed by late fall, apart from ski resorts.

- **National Parks:** Plitvice Lakes and Krka waterfalls can be magical in winter mist or early spring bloom—but trails may be muddy, and services limited.

What Off-Season Travel Requires

If you're traveling outside summer, flexibility is your friend. Call ahead to confirm restaurant hours, museum openings, and transport schedules. Pack a good rain layer and warm clothing, even if you're sticking to the coast. A rental car is more valuable in winter, when public transport options are fewer.

The reward? Fewer crowds, slower pace, and a better sense of how people actually live here. Villages welcome you more openly, and even touristy cities like Dubrovnik reveal their quieter, more authentic side.

12.4 Eco-Friendly Gear Checklist

Why It Matters Here

Croatia and Montenegro both rely heavily on their natural beauty to attract travelers. From the blue-green bays of the Adriatic to the wild trails of Prokletije, tourism here is deeply tied to nature. But with growing crowds and shifting climate patterns, local ecosystems—especially coastal and alpine—are under pressure.

Being a low-impact traveler isn't about perfection. It's about making thoughtful choices: packing gear that reduces waste, supports local communities, and protects the landscapes you're exploring. Many of these choices start before you even leave home.

Reusable Essentials

Single-use plastics are a growing concern across the Balkans. Croatia banned many plastic items in 2021, and Montenegro has begun its own transition, especially in national parks and protected areas. Help keep waste out of the sea and trails by bringing:

- Reusable water bottle: Tap water is safe to drink almost everywhere. Refill often—especially in national parks and on hiking trails.

- Cloth shopping bag: Great for markets, bakeries, and roadside fruit stands.

- Utensil kit: Bamboo or stainless steel forks, knives, and straws reduce waste at picnics or beach takeaways.

- Dry bag or wet pouch: Protects electronics on boat trips or beach days and reduces your need for plastic bags.

Sustainable Clothing & Footwear

Fast fashion has a huge footprint. Instead of buying new outfits for your trip, pack durable clothes you already know and trust. If you're shopping before departure, look for:

- Quick-dry, odor-resistant fabrics (they reduce laundry needs)
- Merino wool layers (natural, breathable, less stink)
- Well-made sandals or hiking shoes that won't fall apart mid-trail

Avoid "disposable" footwear—cheap flip-flops or sandals are often left behind or break quickly on rocky terrain. Local waste systems aren't equipped to handle a flood of abandoned tourist gear.

Toiletries Without the Trash

Many Adriatic towns have aging sewer systems, especially on the islands. That means what goes down the drain matters. Biodegradable, ocean-safe toiletries are a small shift with a big impact.

Consider packing:

- Solid shampoo and conditioner bars
- Refillable travel-size containers
- Reef-safe sunscreen (free of oxybenzone and octinoxate)
- Menstrual cups or washable period underwear (great for long hikes or rural stays)

Toilet paper should never be flushed in older buildings or ferry bathrooms. Always dispose of it in the bin, and carry a small packet of tissues just in case.

Low-Impact Hiking and Adventure Gear

If you're exploring nature reserves or highland trails, take only what you need—and leave no trace. Some useful eco-conscious additions:

- Compact trash pouch: Carry your own litter out of parks and beaches. Bonus if you pick up extra.

- Solar power bank: Keeps your devices charged without relying on extra plug time in remote areas.

- Local trail maps: Download offline maps or pick up regional hiking guides instead of over-relying on signal-dependent apps.

Some national parks have strict rules about campfires, trail use, or drone flying. Read signage carefully, and ask rangers if you're unsure.

Supporting Local, Not Landfill

Eco-friendly travel isn't just about what you avoid—it's also about what you support. When you do buy something, try to choose items made by local artisans, farmers, or small producers. Whether it's handmade soap in Korčula or beeswax wraps in Cetinje, these small purchases support sustainable local economies and cut down on imported packaging.

A good rule: if it's made of plastic and covered in branding, it probably won't make a meaningful souvenir—and might not last the flight home.

Final Thoughts: Balance Over Perfection

You don't have to be an expert environmentalist to travel thoughtfully in Croatia and Montenegro. Every small decision—bringing a bottle, reusing a towel, buying local honey instead of imported snacks—adds up. These countries are still early in their transition toward eco-conscious tourism. Visitors who lead by example can help set a tone for more sustainable exploration in the years ahead.

Chapter 13: Beyond the Map – Insider Tips

Every good trip has its planned moments: the museum you looked up months ago, the restaurant that came highly recommended, the hotel with the view. But what often makes a trip memorable are the unplanned surprises—a quiet hilltop with no one else around, a local trick to skip the long line, a free wine tasting you happened to walk into. This chapter is about exactly those moments. It's packed with practical strategies and lesser-known gems to help you go beyond what's in the brochures.

Here you'll find tools to stretch your travel budget without cutting corners, ways to avoid common fees and headaches, scenic corners not pinned on every travel map, and ideas for giving back meaningfully to the places you visit. Whether you're trying to dodge Dubrovnik's cruise ship crowds or simply want your photos to look like more than postcards, these insights can help you travel smarter, slower, and with a deeper connection to the places you pass through.

13.1 Budget Hacks & Tourist-Tax Strategies

When "Budget Travel" Doesn't Mean Cutting Comfort

Traveling in Croatia and Montenegro on a budget isn't just for backpackers or students. With a little planning, you can eat well, sleep in beautiful places, and explore thoroughly—without overspending. The key is understanding how local systems work: where costs are inflated, when fees apply, and how to avoid paying more than you need to for the same experience.

It's not about cutting corners. It's about knowing where not to spend.

Avoiding the Tourist Tax Trap

Both Croatia and Montenegro charge tourist taxes—daily fees that vary by location and accommodation type. These taxes are usually modest (a few euros per person per night), but they can add up over longer stays. In most formal lodgings (hotels, guesthouses, apartments), the tax is already included in your rate, but not always. Double-check before booking, and ask directly at check-in if the tax is separate.

In Montenegro, hosts are legally required to register foreign guests with the local tourist office. This applies even for private apartments or Airbnb-style rentals. Registration is usually free for you, but failure to do it could result in fines for your host—and awkward situations for you. Politely confirm your host has handled the paperwork.

Some travelers try to avoid these taxes by camping informally or staying off-grid. Be cautious: unregistered lodging is technically illegal and can be risky, especially in national parks or coastal zones where patrols are more frequent in summer.

Saving on Transportation

Transportation is one of the easiest areas to overspend if you don't plan ahead. Taxis in tourist-heavy zones—especially around ferry ports, border crossings, and airports—can be costly. Instead, use local bus lines when possible. Croatia's intercity bus system is excellent and reasonably priced. Montenegro's is more limited but manageable for coastal travel.

Consider this: A bus ride from Dubrovnik to Kotor can cost a fraction of what a private transfer would, and the views are still spectacular. If you're renting a car, compare pickup/drop-off fees—one-way rentals across borders are expensive. Returning your car in the same country (and ideally the same city) can cut costs dramatically.

Avoid fuel surcharges by refueling at larger, inland stations instead of coastal ones, which often have higher prices for the tourist traffic.

Local Markets, Bakery Wisdom & Meal Timing

Croatia and Montenegro have strong local food cultures, and eating well doesn't mean dining out every meal. Local bakeries (pekara in Croatian and Montenegrin) are your best friends. A warm burek or fresh pastry makes a filling breakfast or snack for just a few euros. Many towns hold daily or weekly open-air markets where you can stock up on fruit, cheese, olives, and cured meats. For a picnic lunch with a view, this beats a sit-down restaurant any day.

Dinner is the priciest meal in most restaurants. Consider having your main meal earlier in the day (many places serve lunch specials known as *marenda* in Croatia). If you're renting an apartment, even cooking a few simple meals with local ingredients can be both satisfying and budget-friendly.

And when you do go out, ask for the house wine—it's usually local, affordable, and perfectly good.

Smart Sightseeing & Fee-Free Finds

Many of the most iconic sites—fortresses, churches, viewpoints—come with entry fees. But there are often just-as-impressive alternatives nearby that don't. Instead of entering Dubrovnik's City Walls (a stunning but pricey experience), you could hike Mount Srđ for free and get a panoramic view of the city below. In Kotor, the old fortress stairs are officially ticketed, but locals often point you to alternate trailheads that lead to similar views.

Free walking tours (often tip-based) are available in major cities like Split and Zagreb. They're not only cheaper than guided excursions but also tend to be more personal, with local guides offering honest, unvarnished insights. Just remember to tip fairly—it's how they make their living.

Museums often have free admission days, especially in off-season months. Check cultural calendars or ask at tourist info desks.

Hidden Charges to Watch For

- Cash-only venues: Many local spots still prefer cash, especially in rural or island areas. Avoid ATM fees by withdrawing larger amounts at once. ATMs affiliated with local banks tend to offer better exchange rates than stand-alone machines.

- Currency confusion: As of January 2023, Croatia now uses the euro. Montenegro, though not in the EU, also uses the euro. Don't bother changing money into kuna or other currencies—just carry euros and a card that doesn't charge foreign transaction fees.

- City fees for cars: Some old towns restrict vehicle access or require permits for parking. Before booking accommodation with a car, ask exactly where and how you'll park.

13.2 Photo-Worthy Spots & Hidden Viewpoints

Chasing the Iconic Shot—Without the Crowd

Let's be honest: part of travel today is photography. Whether you're a serious photographer or just trying to take great vacation photos, Croatia and Montenegro offer no shortage of breathtaking scenery. But many "famous" viewpoints—like Dubrovnik's city walls, Kotor's fortress, or Plitvice's wooden boardwalks—are crowded from dawn to dusk in summer.

There are still plenty of places where you can get that postcard-perfect view *and* have it mostly to yourself. You just have to be a little creative—or get there earlier than everyone else.

Dubrovnik Beyond the Walls

Everyone flocks to Dubrovnik's Old Town, and rightly so. But if you want sweeping views without the elbow-to-elbow experience, consider heading up Mount Srđ for sunrise. You can hike the trail (about an hour) or take the cable car and walk a few extra minutes to the Napoleonic fortress ruins. Fewer people go early in the day, and the light on the terracotta rooftops is worth the wake-up call.

Alternatively, take a sea kayak along the outer walls at golden hour. The view looking back toward the town from the water is unforgettable—and most day-tour groups have already left by then.

Kotor's Hidden Paths

The fortress trail above Kotor is a rite of passage for many travelers, but it's also heavily trafficked. Instead of using the main staircase from the old town, find the *Ladder of Kotor*—a zigzag trail that locals use, which begins outside the north gate. It takes longer but is quieter and offers better views of the bay, especially near the tiny chapel of St. Giovanni.

For another perspective, take a short boat ride to the small fishing village of Prčanj across the bay. The view back toward Kotor is just as dramatic—and rarely photographed.

Offbeat Adriatic Vistas

- Ston's City Walls: Far less crowded than Dubrovnik's and equally photogenic, especially at sunset with the salt pans and hills behind you.

- Vis Island's Fort George: Abandoned and a bit rugged, this 19th-century British fort offers killer views and almost no tourists. Bring a picnic.

- Lake Skadar (Montenegro): The horseshoe bend near Rijeka Crnojevića is a classic drone spot, but also stunning from a simple roadside turnout.

- Biokovo Skywalk: Perched above the Makarska Riviera, this glass viewing platform gives vertigo-inducing views of the sea and islands far below. Go early in the morning or late afternoon to avoid glare and crowds.

Tips for Better Travel Photography

- Golden hours matter: Sunrise and sunset provide softer light, fewer tourists, and better contrast. Midday sun tends to wash out colors—especially near the coast.

- Be patient: Wait a few minutes for a crowd to clear, or move slightly to change your angle. A 10-minute wait can mean the difference between a great photo and a mediocre one.

- Zoom with your feet: Walk around the scene. The most striking images often come from surprising angles—not the obvious ones.

- Get lost a little: Some of the best photo spots aren't marked or recommended. Wander up staircases in small towns like Perast or Primošten, and you'll stumble on quiet balconies and alleys with painterly views.

13.3 Volunteer Travel & Giving Back

Traveling With a Purpose

Volunteering while traveling isn't just about altruism—it's about connection. It offers a way to engage with a destination beyond sightseeing, and to contribute meaningfully to the communities that welcome you. In Croatia and Montenegro, opportunities for responsible, local-level volunteering are steadily growing. From marine conservation efforts on the Adriatic to cultural preservation in remote mountain villages, there are ways to give back that don't feel like performative tourism or token gestures.

This part of your journey may not appear on a standard itinerary, but it can become one of the most rewarding parts of the trip.

What Volunteering Looks Like Here

Volunteering in Croatia and Montenegro isn't as institutionalized as it might be in parts of Southeast Asia or Latin America. You won't find major volunteer-tourism hubs, and that's actually a good thing. Most legitimate opportunities are run by grassroots organizations or small NGOs that prefer longer stays, hands-on help, and a willingness to live simply.

In Croatia, marine biology centers along the Dalmatian Coast sometimes accept short-term volunteers to assist with turtle rehabilitation or beach-cleaning initiatives. On Vis and Lastovo, two of the less-developed islands, you may come across permaculture farms or olive groves that welcome seasonal help in exchange for room and board. These aren't "luxury voluntourism" gigs—they're rustic, real-world exchanges.

Montenegro, especially around Lake Skadar and Durmitor, sees small-scale conservation work focused on bird habitats, clean water advocacy, and sustainable farming. Cultural initiatives in places like Cetinje or the mountain hamlets of Prokletije seek help preserving oral histories, restoring abandoned homes, or supporting youth programs in areas at risk of depopulation.

Finding Responsible Projects

The best volunteering projects are often found through word-of-mouth or local networks, not flashy websites. Ask guesthouse owners, national park staff, or community centers if they know of any opportunities. Some hostels and eco-lodges collaborate with NGOs or offer work-exchange programs—helping with gardening, reception, or trail maintenance in exchange for a bed and meals.

Avoid programs that require hefty fees up front without clearly explaining how your money is used. Ethical programs will be transparent about their goals, who benefits, and how your presence contributes.

If you're interested in more structured involvement, check for temporary positions with established networks like WWOOF (World Wide Opportunities on Organic Farms) or work-exchange platforms—but vet each host carefully, especially in rural areas where standards and expectations may vary.

Ways to Give Back Without Volunteering Full-Time

Not everyone has the time—or the energy—for full volunteering stints, especially on shorter trips. That doesn't mean you can't contribute.

Support community-based tourism: Choose a homestay in an inland village rather than an anonymous apartment in a tourist-heavy city. Buy souvenirs directly from artisans rather than airport shops. Spend your money in family-owned konobas and mountain huts rather than global chains.

Consider donating to reputable local conservation groups. Organizations like Green Action Croatia (Zelena Akcija) or EXPEDITIO Montenegro work on everything from environmental protection to heritage preservation. A small donation goes further than you think.

Even small acts—picking up trash on a hiking trail, tipping generously at a family-run guesthouse, or giving honest reviews for small businesses—can make a difference.

Giving with Humility and Respect

The most important thing when giving back is to be thoughtful about the impact. Don't assume that because you're helping, your presence is always welcome. Volunteer roles should serve the community, not your resume or Instagram.

Be willing to listen more than you speak. Learn a few local phrases. Be on time. Ask questions before assuming anything.

Respect that you are a guest in someone else's home, country, and culture.

True connection—like true travel—starts with curiosity and respect.

13.4 Future-Proof Travel Amid Rising Tourism

A Changing Region

The Adriatic coastline, once a low-key collection of fishing towns and sun-soaked villages, has changed dramatically in recent years. Dubrovnik saw a surge in visitors after *Game of Thrones*. Kotor's cruise ship arrivals jumped after its UNESCO status became widely known. Even lesser-known islands are beginning to feel the impact of tourism—both its benefits and its pressure points.

As more people arrive, the region is adjusting: prices are going up, infrastructure is evolving, and locals are debating how to balance preservation with prosperity. For travelers, this shift means rethinking how we move through a place.

Not just how to see it—but how to leave it better than we found it.

Understanding the Impact

Overtourism is no longer just a buzzword—it's a lived reality in cities like Split and Dubrovnik, particularly during July and August. The surge strains waste systems, prices out locals, and risks damaging the cultural fabric that made these places appealing in the first place.

Meanwhile, inland and lesser-visited areas struggle to attract support. Villages in central Croatia or northern Montenegro often lack the infrastructure to accommodate mass tourism but have incredible cultural and natural assets—wooden churches, local festivals, and rare wildlife habitats.

One future-proof travel habit is simple: spread out your footprint. Spend fewer days in the hotspots, and more time in the under-the-radar places that need your visit more than Dubrovnik's already-crowded streets do.

Traveling Slower, Spending Smarter

Slow travel isn't just a lifestyle choice—it's a sustainability tool. Staying longer in fewer places reduces your transport emissions and deepens your experience. It also funnels money into local economies in a more sustained, meaningful way. Renting a cabin in Gorski Kotar for a week instead of rushing from Split to Plitvice in a day lets you connect with fewer people—but more deeply.

When you do spend money, be intentional. Look for eco-certified lodges, guides who work independently, and businesses that engage with the local community rather than bypassing it. Don't shy away from asking questions like: Where is this food sourced? Who owns this property? It's okay to be a conscious guest.

Respecting Local Rhythms

One underrated part of sustainable travel is simply blending in. Respect local rhythms. Don't arrive loudly at a guesthouse at midnight. Don't drone over private property. Don't touch the frescoes in medieval chapels. These aren't strict rules—they're small actions that show you see the place as more than just a backdrop for your vacation.

You can also support efforts to protect natural and cultural heritage by visiting responsibly managed sites, paying entrance fees where requested, and not going off-trail in protected areas. On Biokovo, for example, erosion from careless hikers has begun to damage alpine plants. On Lake Skadar, feeding or touching pelicans—even if offered by a boat operator—should be avoided. These animals are endangered and need space, not selfies.

Thinking Long-Term

Future-proof travel also means thinking about the long game. That includes your carbon footprint. Ferries are often more efficient than flights between Adriatic hubs—consider traveling by sea between Split and Hvar rather than hopping on a short-haul plane. If you're driving, look into carpooling apps or renting hybrids where possible. Carry a refillable bottle—many towns have public fountains with drinkable water.

It also means preparing for a future where parts of the coast may become more regulated, or even restricted. Cities like Venice and Barcelona are experimenting with tourist entry caps. Dubrovnik has already limited cruise ship arrivals. Getting ahead of the curve means embracing flexibility, supporting thoughtful regulation, and choosing destinations that reward respectful travel.

The Adriatic is not a theme park. It's a living region of farmers, fishers, students, elders, artists, and working people. If we want it to remain vibrant and welcoming into the future, we need to travel with that awareness—and care.

Conclusion

Looking back, and looking forward.

After thousands of kilometers, dozens of islands, centuries-old ruins, mountain roads, coastal cafés, forest trails, ferries, festivals, and sunrises from unfamiliar balconies—you're probably thinking: how do I put it all together? This conclusion won't try to sum up every detail (that's what the chapters are for), but it will help you draw a practical, personal thread through everything you've read. Whether you're deep into planning or just daydreaming about what's possible, this is where we pause to reflect before setting off—or perhaps, returning—on your own terms.

Travel in Croatia and Montenegro isn't about checking things off a list. These countries reward curiosity, patience, and a willingness to go beyond what's easy or obvious. This chapter offers four key takeaways: how to prioritize what matters most to you, how to make your trip truly your own, why slow exploration is worth coming back for, and how we can all help protect what makes the Adriatic special.

Recap Your Priorities: What Kind of Trip Are You Planning?

At this point, you've probably noticed there's no single way to "do" Croatia and Montenegro. These countries hold multitudes: the Adriatic's sea-and-stone rhythms, the medieval stillness of inland monasteries, the pulse of summer music festivals, the scent of rosemary in mountain air, and the quiet pleasure of a meal made by someone's grandmother.

If your goal is to relax, focus on the islands and the slower towns. Southern Dalmatia, the Bay of Kotor, and the Pelješac Peninsula all lend themselves to meandering days and soft evenings. Rent a room near the water, shop in morning markets, and let the days unfold without a schedule.

If you're after history and architecture, carve out time for inland cities and cultural heritage sites. Split, Šibenik, Trogir, Kotor, and Cetinje offer layers of Roman, Venetian, Slavic, and Ottoman influences, all condensed into beautiful, walkable cores.

If you want adventure, go north or go up—into the karst ridges of Paklenica, the rugged beauty of Durmitor, or the wild canyons near Nikšić. Hike, raft, cycle, or drive—just give yourself time to pause between the thrills.

And if you want to mix it all? Good. That's what these countries are built for. The coast and the mountains, the old towns and open roads—they're all closer than they seem. Just allow enough space between destinations to experience them, not just pass through them.

Personalize Your Experience: Make It Yours

No two travelers are the same—and no two itineraries should be either. The best way to personalize your journey is to start with one or two "anchors," then leave some flexibility around them. You might commit to a festival in Zagreb, a kayaking trip in Kotor Bay, or a slow week on Mljet. From there, the rest of the trip can unfold based on mood, conversations, weather, or what catches your eye on the road.

Don't be afraid to say no to "must-sees" that don't interest you. If you'd rather sip wine in Istria than line up outside Dubrovnik's walls at noon, trust your instincts. If you love early mornings and empty trails, build your days around them. Love local food? Prioritize places with traditional konobas and fresh seafood markets. Fascinated by local crafts or music? Look for smaller festivals, museum exhibits, or guided heritage walks, even if they don't appear in glossy brochures.

Your guidebook offers structure, but the best trips are built from the ground up, one conversation and one decision at a time.

Go Deeper—and Come Back

One of the best things about this region is how easy it is to return. You won't "finish" Croatia or Montenegro in one go, and that's a good thing. Maybe you start with the coastline, then return another year to explore the wine valleys inland. Or you spend this summer in the southern bays, then come back in autumn to hike in the Biokovo range or enjoy olive harvests on Brač.

Places change with the seasons and with you. Dubrovnik is one place in July, another entirely in March. Kotor's old town has a different feel under rainclouds than under cruise ship crowds. Even the islands, so idyllic in summer, take on a quiet, local rhythm in October or May—when ferry rides are slower, markets more neighborly, and time seems to stretch.

Think of your first visit not as a box checked but as a beginning. The stories, landscapes, and people here open up more the second—or third—time around.

Final Thoughts: Traveling Light, Leaving a Gentle Footprint

As much as this book has offered practical advice—routes, packing, customs, currencies—what it's really advocating for is a certain kind of travel: thoughtful, flexible, rooted in curiosity and respect.

Tourism is a powerful force in the Adriatic. It sustains families, funds restoration, and helps rural areas survive. But it can also overwhelm fragile ecosystems, erode cultural authenticity, and price locals out of their own cities. Every traveler plays a role in that balance. You don't have to be perfect, just aware.

That means staying in guesthouses where possible. Walking instead of driving when you can. Taking your trash with you. Being respectful in religious or historical sites. Tipping generously when the service feels personal, and giving locals space when they're busy or tired from the long summer season.

And it means remembering that you're not just a visitor—you're a participant. You're part of the daily rhythm, the shared resources, the social fabric, even if just for a few days. Travel is about more than consumption. It's about exchange.

These places are beautiful not just because of their landscapes, but because of the people who live here and the cultures they've carried through centuries of change. If you walk lightly, travel slowly, and stay open to what's around you, they'll reward you with more than you expected—and welcome you again when you return.

Appendix

Helpful extras for planning, packing, and navigating like a pro.

Even with all the chapters behind you, travel still comes down to practical choices—getting from A to B, figuring out what to bring, and knowing what to do if plans shift. This appendix is your final toolkit: a hands-on reference section packed with real-world details to help you navigate, prepare, and troubleshoot on the go. Whether you're about to hit the road or double-checking ferry routes the night before, this is the section to keep bookmarked.

Here you'll find seasonal transit tips, ferry schedules, packing advice tailored to both coastal and inland regions, useful local contact numbers, and a curated list of apps and recommended reading. No filler, no fluff—just clear info for the curious traveler who wants to move smartly, pack wisely, and stay grounded throughout the trip.

A. Transit & Ferry Schedules

Getting around without the guesswork

Croatia and Montenegro offer a mix of old-world charm and modern logistics. While buses and ferries still form the backbone of public transport, they're far more reliable and interconnected than many first-time visitors expect—especially if you know where to look and when to book.

Buses: Intercity and Coastal Routes

In both countries, the regional bus network is extensive and usually dependable. Croatia's main hubs include Zagreb, Split, Zadar, Dubrovnik, and Rijeka, with routes radiating outward to inland villages and seaside towns. Montenegro's key bus terminals are in Podgorica, Herceg Novi, Kotor, Budva, and Nikšić. You'll find frequent buses along the Adriatic coast, particularly in high season. Expect a mix of older coaches and newer models, most with AC and space for luggage.

Tickets can often be purchased at the station window or on board, though it's wise to book ahead online in summer. Buses rarely sell out in the shoulder season (April–May, September–October), and schedules are more forgiving. Just note that "direct" routes may still make local stops. Always confirm travel time before committing to a tight connection.

Ferries: Coastal Islands & Cross-Border Routes

Ferries are a lifeline for island communities and a highlight for many travelers. Croatia has the more developed network, with Jadrolinija operating most major routes. High-season ferries connect Split, Dubrovnik, Šibenik, Zadar, Rijeka, and numerous islands like Brač, Hvar, Korčula, and Vis. The larger car ferries are reliable, but smaller catamarans (passenger only) tend to run faster and serve island-hopping travelers well.

Some key examples:

- Split to Hvar (Stari Grad or Hvar Town): multiple daily ferries, year-round.

- Dubrovnik to Korčula, Mljet, or Lastovo: more frequent May–October.

- Rijeka to Cres and Lošinj: a quieter northern option with scenic crossings.

Montenegro's ferry options are fewer but important. The Kamenari–Lepetane car ferry across the Bay of Kotor runs continuously and takes less than 10 minutes. It's ideal for drivers who want to avoid the long loop around the bay.

Trains: Sparse but Scenic

Croatia's inland rail system connects Zagreb with Osijek, Split, and Rijeka, but isn't ideal for travelers on a tight schedule. It's more useful for exploring the continental interior than coastal areas. Montenegro has a single main line—from Bar to Belgrade, passing through mountainous terrain and dramatic river gorges. If you have time, it's one of the most scenic rail journeys in Europe.

Flights & Regional Airports

Both countries have international airports well-positioned for tourist travel. Zagreb, Split, Dubrovnik, Zadar, and Pula receive seasonal flights from across Europe. In Montenegro, Podgorica and Tivat airports are well-connected in summer, especially from Germany, the UK, and Eastern Europe. Flights within the Balkans are limited, so ground or ferry travel remains the better value.

B. Packing Checklist & Gear Guide

Bring what you need, skip what you don't.

Packing for Croatia and Montenegro means balancing coast and mountain, sun and rain, beachwear and city attire. It's not about stuffing a bag with every possible item—it's about choosing versatile pieces, knowing local expectations, and accounting for where and when you're traveling.

Clothing: Layered and Local-Appropriate

Weather swings between the coastal Adriatic and the inland Dinaric Alps can be dramatic, especially in spring and fall. A summer trip may start in 33°C heat in Dubrovnik and end with a chilly hike in Durmitor. Prioritize light, breathable layers, but always include a windbreaker or fleece—even in July.

Beaches call for swimwear, of course, but keep a lightweight cover-up or linen shirt for cafés and ferry rides. Inland towns, religious sites, and even some restaurants expect slightly more conservative attire, especially for women. Pack at least one outfit that feels polished but still travel-friendly: think long pants or a casual dress, plus a scarf or wrap.

Shoes: Comfort First

Forget heels or stiff dress shoes. What you need are two reliable pairs:

- Sturdy walking shoes or sneakers for towns, cobbled streets, and casual hikes.

- Sandals or quick-drying water shoes for beaches, boat rides, and uneven coastal terrain.

If you're hiking or cycling inland, consider trail shoes or boots with good ankle support. And always break them in before you travel—blisters are harder to manage on the road.

Specialty Gear: Smart Extras

- Dry bag: Great for kayaking, boat trips, or sudden rain.

- Universal sink plug: Useful for doing laundry in hotels or guesthouses.

- Refillable water bottle: Tap water is safe to drink in both countries.

- Compact power bank: Useful for long travel days, especially with ferry delays.

- Flashlight or headlamp: Handy for camping, hiking, or remote villages with limited lighting.

Toiletries & Health

Bring what you're used to, but don't overpack. Pharmacies are widely available, and basics like sunscreen, bug spray, or motion sickness pills are easy to find. For women, tampons and menstrual cups are less available than pads in smaller towns—pack accordingly if that's relevant.

Don't forget travel-size versions of:

- High-SPF sunscreen

- After-sun aloe or lotion

- Bug repellent (especially for evenings inland)

- Basic first-aid (plasters, antiseptic wipes, painkillers)

C. Emergency Contacts & Useful Apps

Be prepared without overthinking it

Most trips through Croatia and Montenegro are smooth sailing. But it's smart to know how to get help if you need it—whether that's for a missed ferry, a twisted ankle on a hiking trail, or simply getting lost in the old town after dark. This section pulls together the key phone numbers, embassy info, and mobile apps that can save time, reduce stress, or even help in a real emergency.

Emergency Numbers (Quick Dial)

Both Croatia and Montenegro use the 112 number for general emergencies—this works across the EU and Balkan region. It connects you to police, fire, and medical assistance in English or the local language. Here are the most relevant direct numbers as well:

Croatia:

- Police: 192
- Fire: 193
- Ambulance: 194
- Roadside assistance (HAK): +385 1 1987

Montenegro:

- Police: 122
- Fire: 123
- Ambulance: 124
- Roadside help (AMSCG): +382 20 234 999

Most people speak at least some English, especially in tourist areas, but it's helpful to have your location info ready (cross streets, landmarks, or GPS pins if possible).

Health & Pharmacy Access

In both countries, pharmacies (apoteka) are widely available and can assist with common ailments—headaches, allergies, sunburns, motion sickness, etc. In major cities and tourist centers, many are open late or even 24/7. Hospital care is generally high quality, especially in Croatia, which is part of the EU system. Travelers from Europe should bring their EHIC/GHIC card; others should carry proof of travel insurance.

Embassy and Consular Services

It's unlikely you'll need your country's embassy, but it's wise to note down locations in case of lost passports or legal issues. Most embassies are based in Zagreb (Croatia) or Podgorica (Montenegro), with some consulates in cities like Split and Dubrovnik. Many offer online appointment booking. Always store a digital and physical copy of your passport, insurance, and visa documents.

Useful Mobile Apps

You don't need to overload your phone, but a few reliable apps can genuinely improve your trip. No sales pitch—just real-world tools travelers have come to rely on.

- Rome2Rio (route planning): Good for checking bus/ferry/train connections.

- Moovit (local transit): Useful for navigating Zagreb, Split, and Podgorica.

- Google Translate (with Croatian & Montenegrin downloaded offline).

- Maps.me or AllTrails: For offline hiking maps in Durmitor, Biokovo, and national parks.

- Jadrolinija app (Croatia ferries): Real-time ferry schedules and ticket options.

- WhatsApp: Widely used by guesthouses and tour guides for quick communication.

- AirVisual or Plume: Handy during wildfires (late summer) to check air quality.

- XE Currency: For checking Kuna (HRK), Euro (EUR), or other

exchanges easily.

Bonus tip: Set up your phone with eSIM or a local SIM card if you plan to stay longer than a week or want fast mobile data. Croatian and Montenegrin providers offer tourist packages with generous data limits at low prices.

Printed in Dunstable, United Kingdom